TENNER THOMPSON

By the same author:—

INTO THE SAME IMAGE
THEY TEACH US TO PRAY
PRAYER IS THE SECRET

Beneath the Cross of Jesus

Meditations on the Passion of our Lord

by

REGINALD E. O. WHITE   M.A., B.D.

Wm. B. Eerdmans Publishing Company
Grand Rapids, Michigan

Library of Congress Catalog Card Number: 59-14587

Printed in the United States of America

First edition, October 1959

CONTENTS

CONSIDERATIONS THAT ENRICH DEVOTION

PARADOXES THAT PROVOKE REFLECTION

The attraction that repels
The strength of weakness
The peril of security
The hurt that heals
The timeless hour
The failure that succeeds

1 The Attraction that Repels

"The offence of the cross. . . ."
"And I, if I be lifted up from the earth, will draw all men unto me."

Galatians 5:11, John 12:32

THE CHRISTIAN SYMBOL has become, through centuries of devotion, the object of profound reverence; but neither poetry, nor art, nor the gold and jewels of the craftsman can wholly disguise the fact that crucifixion was a dreadful form of execution. The ancients themselves describe it as "a most cruel and most horrible torture". The faith which sets out to conquer the world with a gibbet on its banner proves its fundamental realism, whatever charges of "opiate" or "wishful thinking" may be made against it. For the cross *offends*, and always will.

To the Greek mind, the cross was merely incomprehensible. That men should be "saved" by it was preposterous; that men should preach it, sheer foolishness. "The world by wisdom knew not God" and had found no way of world salvation. The message of the cross underlined that failure; it called for simplicity of faith, not intellectual cleverness; and it perpetually recalled what human "wisdom" did with such a One as Christ. To the Greek therefore the whole idea of redemptive suffering was manifold folly.

To the Jew, a crucified Messiah was scandalous; a given, free and universal salvation, an attack upon his privileged security. Proudly the Jew proclaimed the divine election of his race and the sufficiency of the Law; the cross of Jesus, as the only hope for all mankind, was double blasphemy. Many things can alienate men from God, but if humility find the way to penitence all can be overcome — but pride. "God *resisteth* the proud" and giveth His grace to contrite hearts humble enough to rest their hope wholly upon Christ's doing for us what we could never hope to have done for themselves.

The offence of the cross is therefore not surprising. To seek to change a man is to imply something unsatisfactory in his present mode of life. You cannot convert him by admiring what he is already: you have to disturb him, challenge, convict and

9

undermine him. It is impossible to save a man without humbling him, to save him from his pride; and subduing him, to save him from his folly. The preaching of the cross pays sinful man no compliments, except indeed the supreme compliment that God thinks he is worth saving. Inevitably therefore the scandal of the passion is the great theme of the evangelist: the scandal of what men did to Jesus, of what God permitted to be done, of what Jesus had to do to save, of what men needed should be done. The offer of free pardon leaves man nothing to be but grateful, nothing to do but accept. And impenitent men do not like it. To that extent you cannot save a man without offending him, though it is not for us to multiply offence by clumsy speech or lack of courtesy.

Yet is it also true you cannot save a man without attracting him. The method of the gospel is neither condemnation, fear nor force, but a new, divine fascination, the kindling of desire, the awakening of love. If you cannot change a soul without implying censure of his present way of life, neither can you do it against his will. It is essential that his heart be won; and a long — and lengthening — roll of the redeemed bear witness to the appeal of Calvary. The "offensive" cross is nevertheless the magnet of the world. "I, if I be lifted up from the earth, will *draw* all men unto me."

Nor can this be thought surprising. If the whole race instinctively understands anything, it is suffering, sin, and love; and these three spell out plainly all the message of the cross.

All men know suffering, in every age and race. It appeals to natural sympathy: the suffering of the brave especially so, the suffering of the good man most of all. Calvary speaks unambiguously to a world in pain.

All men know sin, too. It appeals to the intuitive sense of right and wrong, interpreting the world's dark experience of lust and evil, remorse and fear. Calvary speaks unmistakably to a world wrestling with evil.

And all men know love. It appeals to the universal loneliness that lies within our secret selves, the longing for friendship adequate to help, able to understand. Deep within human nature stirs a hunger for divine companionship, and the cross speaks persuasively to a world in need of love.

10

The appeal is felt at each stage of life. In youth suffering numbs; in manhood it can embitter; in age it may despair. In youth sin frightens; in manhood it enslaves; in age it takes revenge. In youth the want of love confuses; in manhood it makes cynical; in age it crushes utterly. But youth, manhood, age find answer in the message of the cross.

Suffering, sin and love is the ABC of the world's long story, the theme of all great literature, subject of all great painting, key to all great music. This is the real eternal triangle, and at its apex stands the cross of Jesus. For there He suffered as none has ever suffered, to show the suffering of God for a world astray; He bore sin as none other ever could, to bring men back to God; He loved as none has ever loved, to show the love of God.

No wonder the upraised Christ draws all men unto Him. George Young tells of his Chinese teacher, Mr. Lu, at first disdainful of this strange foreign tale of a peasant born within a stable. His interest quickened at the Master's teaching, but still Confucius was superior. The parable of the prodigal moved him to confess, "I did not know God was like that". But the story of the passion reduced him to silence, and the language lesson ended with a whispered, "Why did He die like that?", and George Young's answer in imperfect Chinese, "He died for me — and you". Wrapping his books in his blue cloth Mr. Lu went out, deeply troubled: he returned next day a different man, to say, "Mr. Young, I have become a disciple of your Jesus!"

So the magnetism of the cross still holds. Above the little iron churches of the Congo forest the slender symbol rises; within great shrines or simple halls, in camp and hospital and quiet place, the Table of remembrance stands, witnessing that the attraction abides, that speaking all men's language the cross has said rememberable things men longed to hear.

Yet it repels. The cross of Jesus woos some to salvation, warns others of judgment. We do well to come to terms with this paradox of Calvary, both in our evangelism and in ourselves. For the explanation lies in the difference in people.

For some, light-hearted, unconcerned, the cross *must* be repulsive, irrelevant, unwanted, a stark reminder of all that darker side of life from which most modern people resolutely turn away. Not all our new techniques of evangelistic approach can ever make the passion of our Lord a popular theme. To the crowd, it still is "folly".

But for others, hungering and thirsting after righteousness, in earnest about life and realistic about death, in whose hearts deep thought and dark experience have sharpened understanding, Calvary has meaning and value and eternal radiance. To such it is the fountain of worship, the hope of the world, the spearhead of the Christian message, the motive of sublimest character, the soul's deepest comfort, the heart's only legitimate pride.

Thus in His death the Master sifts the hearts of men. Beneath His cross the paths divide. Some, repelled, hurry away with scornful smile, or angry frown, or uneasy mind: others remain to wonder, to worship, and to pray. Either way the cross provokes response. What shall be ours?

2 The Strength of Weakness

*"They laid hold upon one Simon, a Cyrenian, coming out of
the country, and on him they laid the cross, that he might bear
it after Jesus."*
"He was crucified through weakness."
"The weakness of God is stronger than men."
"When I am weak, then am I strong."

Luke 23:26, II Corinthians 13:4, I Corinthians 1:25,
II Corinthians 12:10

IT IS USUALLY ASSUMED that Simon of Cyrene was compelled to
carry the cross because Jesus had fallen exhausted beneath its
weight. The strain of previous days, the long sleepless night,
the hostile cross-examination, the mockery and the terrible Roman
scourging sufficiently explain Christ's weakness, and the early
death which surprised experienced Pilate. The suggestion is con-
firmed by the cry of compassion which, as Luke says at this
point, the women of Jerusalem set up for His extremity of suffering.

This physical exhaustion of Jesus is probably part at least
of what Paul has in mind in the strange, unwelcome words, "He
was crucified through weakness." As Jesus stands before the
crowd, with bound hands and torn brow, and even Pilate pleads
their pity for Him, He seems so utterly vulnerable, so completely
at the mercy of priests and people, soldiers and governor — a
lonely, silent, meek and helpless Figure, friendless and unde-
fended. Truly He was crucified through weakness.

But even as you contemplate that forlorn picture, you become
aware of another that stands behind it, drawn upon a larger canvas and suggesting deeper truth. All through His ministry Jesus
had confronted the powers of this world with weapons that seemed
impossibly puny, and with strength that seemed incredibly inadequate. Backing Pilate was Rome, mistress of the world, whose
legions marched from India to the Atlantic, whose writ ran in
every court and senate house around the Mediterranean. Backing Caiaphas was Jewry, entrenched in ancient religion, fervent

13

nationalism, intense conviction, a proud and wealthy aristocracy, a sense of divinely ordained superiority, all maintained by skilful and resolute diplomacy. And, for the while at least, backing both is another fearful power in human affairs, the clamour of the mob.

Facing them is Jesus, personifying all that seemingly can never hope to conquer — simplicity and truth, humility and gentleness, idealism that will not stoop to use of arms or worldly means, but pursues its way in childlike faith and love until the forces of this world break it on some cross. This is His story, and the story of saints and martyrs in all ages; truth, right and goodness seem ever weak and frail and vulnerable; falsehood and wrong seem mighty, and have their way.

Yet behind that picture, we might almost say, there stands a third, dimly and astonishingly suggested in words we scarcely like to take too seriously. In a glowing passage, where the ardour of the writer transforms argument almost into poetry, and certainly into rhetoric, Paul declares that "the foolishness of God is wiser than men, and the weakness of God is stronger than men". "The weakness of God" — even allowing for the warmth of argument, it is a startling phrase.

Paul dares to compare the strength of God and man, and to suggest that God, even at His weakest — even when limited, hedged about, restrained, as it were, by mercy and gentleness and truth, even though He still respects the freedom of the souls He made, and stoops to plead, to wait, and woo — still God, in the restraining of His strength and the withholding of His power, is mightier than the mighty and stronger than the strong, and shall prevail.

It is a daring thought, but Paul is thinking of the cross, as the context shows. There, so to speak, God is seen willingly at His weakest, suffering, submitting, and rejected; yet that same cross is the power of God unto salvation. They scorned and rejected, smote and scourged, crowned and crucified, yet He broke them in the doing of it, broke them, outdid them, and conquered them. As the Scottish preacher cried, "Where now are all those who put my Lord to death? Either at His feet, or under them!"

This is a part of the paradox of the passion, this mighty weakness of the dying Christ. Never was suffering more triumphant, silence more eloquent, love more powerful, meekness so mighty; never was submission so plainly the way to mastery, truth rejected so unanswerable, exhaustion so near omnipotence. He was crucified through weakness, and lives by the power of God. There is a moral here for drooping faith. This, Paul immediately argues, is ever God's way, choosing the weak things of the world to confound the things that are mighty. The mills of God grind noiselessly, and the forces that make for righteousness and victory often use seemingly weak men for their agents and apparent defeat for their instrument.

In nature, as we know, God loves to work by imperceptible ways.

The innocent moon, that nothing does but shine,
Moves all the labouring surges of the world.

The silent, secret, irresistible forces of the deepening frost can fracture iron and split the hardest stone. Gently and silently, all about us in the springtime, moves that rising tide of life that will clothe the woods with leaves, the fields with corn, and bring back the beauty and the song of summer. Even so God works in history. The mightiest forces are abroad in the weak and silent movements of the world.

And they matter. A party of Arctic travellers — so runs the tale — fighting their way northward against blizzard and bitter weather, seemed to get no nearer to their goal. The whole, vast snow-covered ice-cap on which they trudged was itself drifting slowly, almost imperceptibly southward, caught in an unmarked current of the polar seas. All their labour went for nothing against the secret, silent movement of their world, until they changed to another, northward moving floe. Time and the will of God move steadily onwards: it's a great comfort to be going God's way. It is a heartening faith, this confidence in unseen forces that operate through agencies that the world may scorn. Few can rise to it as Paul did, finding contentment in his weakness and a spur in his handicap, glorying in his infirmity that the power of Christ might rest the more fully upon him. "For when I am weak, then am I strong."

15

But there is more within this paradox than a lesson on encouragement; there is challenging truth for those who would dismiss the passion-story as an old religious tale. For in the history of mankind that cross of weakness has proved mightier than the marching legions and stronger than the sword.

Would you measure strength by its *endurance?* The reed sceptre of Jesus has outlasted the rod that Pilate carried; the purple robe with which they mocked Him has long outworn the High Priest's garment; His crown of thorns has kept its evergreen, while Caesar's chaplet is no more; the succession of Christ's followers attended the mighty legions to their tomb.

Or would you measure strength by its *resistance?* The message of the cross is set inevitably against the intellectual pride of mere philosophy, the religious pride of those who think to save themselves, the sentimentalism of those who will not face the fact of sin. Its self-denying challenge is unwelcome in an age of pleasure and slack discipline; its call to sacrifice offends the selfishness of unregenerate hearts. Even its glorious invitation to be reconciled to God falls often upon ears unheeding any music but the raucous babble of the world. Yet, confronting though it does with warning and hard truth the weakness and the sins of men, never has the cross yet lacked for those in whom it has conquered evil and enthroned the Christ.

Or would you measure strength by its *achievement?* The dying Christ has changed the face of Europe, girdled the world with His name, gathered in all ages a multitude of earth's noblest souls. The crucified Saviour kindled in society a force of inspiration that burst upon the world in glorious architecture, inspired music, stirring poetry, and eloquent art. For His sake, men have suffered, striven and endured, and for His glory in mankind's good men have lived and died.

From men's love of Him have flowed a thousand creative impulses to succour the needy, befriend the oppressed, attempt great enterprise and uproot ancient wrongs. Innumerable souls unite with Paul to testify that though He was crucified through weakness, yet when we were without strength He died for the ungodly, and out of weakness we are made strong.

This is the crowning significance of the paradox. When all the embattled forces of the world's great powers conspired against the Christ, to crush His gentle frailty in their ruthless hands,

He who had not strength to carry His cross bent them to His purpose. For with that cross for lever, and the conscience of the race for fulcrum, God still raises men from shame and death to life and glory, and will yet lift the world.

3 The Peril of Security

"If we let him thus alone . . . the Romans shall come and take away both our place and nation. . . . It is expedient for us, that one man should die for the people, and that the whole nation perish not."
"We shall be saved from wrath . . . who have fled for refuge."

John 11:48, 50, Romans 5:9, Hebrews 6:18

To A GENERATION that has seen so many heroic deeds, so much of adventure, and of peril courageously outfaced, it is perhaps natural that the gospel of Christ should seem too concerned with safety. It invites young men and women to be "saved", when the emphasis in almost every other field of thought is on willingness to take risks, to dare, to venture, to climb the unclimbed mountains, to control immeasurable forces, to explore the unexplored poles, to range the untravelled spaces, to move at incredible speeds where life and death hang upon split-second decisions.

Our generation has shown no lack of physical courage, or intellectual daring. Blood and toil and tears and sweat found us afraid, but unflinching: thousands train for tasks that involve personal peril, even, in the new sciences, lingering mutilation, with the cool and long-drawn bravery of the bomb-disposal squad. Is it really any wonder that we no longer sing

> Safe in the arms of Jesus,
> Safe on His gentle breast,

or if we do, that a great many modern folk look askance at us?

Perhaps we have too often given the impression that Christian faith is a way of escape from the dangers of life — and nothing more. "O safe and happy shelter!" "In the secret of His presence how my soul delights to hide." Some of us know, out of a troubled experience, the truths that lie enshrined in such expressions, but is that the whole of the Christian invitation?

On wider planes of thought, the idea has possessed us all. We offer Christ to young people as the Guardian and Keeper who will shield them from the world's blasts and preserve them

from all evil. Did not Christ let Peter face the danger, and the
fall, that he might grow stronger?

So we promise a world safe for spiritual things, a world secure
for our children, if men will come to Christ. Of course, we
want it, and He would grant it if men would. But is that all
we have to say — basing faith on the underlying *fears* of men,
and appealing to something that the world cannot distinguish
from moral cowardice, the infant's longing to be sheltered, well-
wrapped up, and safe?

Of course it would be stupid to despise this note of the
gospel. There are perils which a man is simply foolish to face
unprotected; and sin is one of them. There are emergencies of
the soul that man is mad to go unprepared for; and temptation
is one of them. There are crises of experience which no man
would want to face without God; and death is one of them.
Death, and

> *the dread of something after death,*
> *The undiscover'd country from whose bourn*
> *No traveller returns, ...*
> *Thus conscience does make cowards of us all. . . .*

The man who has found no inner citadel of safety, whose soul
stands wide open to the blustering storms of life, who knows no
refuge of faith, no strong tower of prayer, no encircling walls of
habitual piety, no underlying arms of love, is a man to be
pitied indeed. He is not strong, though he thinks he is: he
is vulnerable, and undermined, frail, and at the mercy of all evil.

There is sin, and death, and judgement: the peril that threatens
the present life and the reckoning of the life to come. It is
in that context that the gospel speaks of safety, and safety
through the cross. "A man shall be as an hiding place from
the wind, and a covert from the tempest; as rivers of water in
a dry place, as the shadow of a great rock in a weary land" —
so runs the ancient promise. "I am the door for the sheep," says
Jesus of God's fold, "by me if any man enter in he shall be
safe." "He is able to keep you from falling" is the testimony of
one who had served Him long: "We shall be saved from wrath
through him".

"We have fled for refuge", and have found it: we know no other —

> *None other Lamb, none other Name,*
> *None other hope in heaven or earth or sea,*
> *None other hiding place from guilt and shame,*
> *None beside Thee!*

But it is not all we found. Indeed, that same cross which has proved a place of shelter to countless souls is itself the Christian's sharpest lesson against loving security for its own sake. The story of Christ's passion drives that home with quite astonishing emphasis.

For each of the foremost actors in the drama of Christ's death was striving to find security. The chief priests and the Pharisees, in their council, said: "If we let him thus alone, the Romans shall come and take away both our place and nation". Caiaphas uses the argument: "It is expedient for us, that one man should die for the people, and that the whole nation perish not". Pilate too: "If thou let this man go thou art not Caesar's friend: he that maketh himself a king speaketh against Caesar". The Roman governor understood the threat, and to save himself yielded Jesus up to death. The only intelligible human motive which makes the action of Judas comprehensible is that by betraying Jesus he hoped to save at least his own skin. No one knows if that was in his heart, but it is very likely.

And should we not include Peter also — suddenly afraid, and to save himself taking sides with Christ's enemies.

Is it not significant, that these men who made Christ's Calvary were all men seeking for security? To play for safety all the way — this may *still* put the Christ to death, in your life and mine.

There is a hugging of the shore, in spiritual things, a determination to keep well the right side of enthusiasm; a resolve never to put to sea unless the south wind blows softly, that saps the moral fibre and weakens the conscience. Safety first can be the excuse for slothfulness, the mere shield behind which we hide our disobedience of God's call. In our love of being secure, and seeing all our way, we may crucify Christ's purpose for our lives and miss the best He planned.

The great men of faith were never men for safety first. From Peter, standing in Jerusalem defying the Sanhedrin, down the long line of martyrs, the pioneers of thought and missionary exploration, and the whole sublime succession of the unconsenting conscience who withstood pressures and tortures, fire and death, for truth's sake and for God, they were men who "hazarded their lives". They sought not merely for a refuge, they prayed not merely to be "saved", but that, with hearts safe in Christ's keeping, they might dare flame and passion, fire and steel, and be found faithful unto death.

We simply *must* try to tell our generation this other truth in Christ. There is a *risk* in followng Christ. He asks hard things, He calls to conflict. He will have none of those who look over their shoulder for the safe place and long to hide from the hostility of the world. He offers a cross and a sword: and we betray His challenge — the whole challenge of the spiritual life in a day of easy-going, comfort-loving, fireside religion — if we invite men only to be "safe".

Because, of course, all those who sought security by destroying Him, destroyed themselves. The chief priests saw Jerusalem a heap of rubble; soon Jewry as a national unit ceased to be; Pilate died in exile and disgrace not long after Jesus; Judas went and hanged himself; Peter went out into darkness, weeping bitterly. When you choose security, in preference to right, it is wiser in the long run to reckon seriously with God.

This, surely, is the ultimate word on the whole matter. There *is* no safety but in submission to the truth; there is no security but in obedience to the will of God; there can be no shelter but in surrender to a Saviour able to keep. But submission, obedience, surrender, are no escape from conflict and toil, from risk, and heartache and even sorrow. For the same cross which is our refuge is also our badge of spiritual warfare; and the invitation to be saved is at the same time a challenge to give ourselves "to strive, to seek, to find, and not to yield".

Those who put our Lord to death, seeking security, lost it; He who cared not for it, was safe at last in the Father's hands. Written in blood into the very story of the passion is His own warning against loving security too well: that he that saveth his life shall lose it, and he that loseth it for My sake, the same shall save it — unto life eternal.

4 The Hurt that Heals

"And one of them smote the servant of the high priest, and cut off his right ear. And Jesus answered and said, Suffer ye thus far. And he touched his ear, and healed him".
"But he was wounded for our transgressions, he was bruised for our iniquities: the chastisement of our peace was upon him; and with his stripes we are healed."

Luke 22:50-51, Isaiah 53:5

FOR THREE YEARS the mighty deeds of Jesus demonstrated the health-giving power of the kingdom of God. Wherever He came, healing and strength, sight and sanity came with Him, and men were whole again.

The final miracle, while not the greatest, is altogether fitting — the healing of the ear of one who served His enemies, performed under the shadow of the cross. Jesus is about to be led away to His own wounding: His time is short, but there is time for tenderness. His brow and hands and feet and side are soon to be pierced, His heart will break: but the lesser wound of a serving man must still receive attention. Standing on the threshold of His passion, He is still the healing Christ.

"He was wounded for our transgressions, he was bruised for our iniquities: the chastisement of our peace was upon him; *and with his stripes we are healed."* Thus already on the ancient page the hurt and the healing stand linked together — His hurt, for a whole world's healing.

The prophets were much concerned with this need of healing. Isaiah sees Judah: "The whole head sick, the whole heart faint . . . wounds and bruises and putrefying sores". Jeremiah complains of those who in serious times dealt in dangerous cures, healing "the wound of the daughter of my people" too lightly. Messiah is foreseen as One bringing good tidings to the afflicted and binding up the brokenhearted and the bruised, the Sun of righteousness arising with healing in His wings. God is "the Lord who healeth thee"; "come, let us return unto the Lord: for he hath torn, and he will heal us; he hath smitten, and he will bind us up".

The New Testament dramatises this truth, in the moving story of the ministry of Jesus. He speaks of Himself as the Physician of men and of sin as a sickness of the human spirit. His gift of health, of wholeness of life, gives its root meaning to the New Testament word "salvation". Elsewhere, the gospel is "sound doctrine" — literally the healthy, health-giving teaching.

In Biblical thought man is a unity of body, soul and spirit; disorder anywhere is disorder of the whole. Our theoretic distinctions are convenient fictions: Scripture speaks with greater realism of the effects of sin, and of salvation, not simply upon the "soul" or "spirit" but upon the total man. "Wilt thou be made whole?" is echoed by "Christ Jesus maketh thee whole" — and the meaning is soundness of life on all levels. Says Peter, of the lame man in Jerusalem: "The faith which is by Him hath given him this *perfect soundness*". That is almost a definition of New Testament salvation.

But Jesus once declared that men would surely say to Him, "Physician, heal *thyself*". Well they might: for the cost of His ministry to others was the suffering of His own heart; it is with His stripes that we are healed. In John's words: "As Moses lifted up the serpent in the wilderness" — that the smitten might find healing — "even so must the Son of man *be lifted up*; that whosoever believeth in him should not perish. . .". The leaves of *that* tree are for the healing of the nations; His are "the unhealed, everlasting wounds that heal the world".

A Cornish village chapel was up for sale: it was bought by the local doctor for use as an extra dispensary! A shrewd observer saw in the transaction something typical of our time: the chapel empty, the doctor's surgery overfull. The loss of faith, and of the inward peace that faith bestows, lies at the root of many maladies of our age.

Our generation is brilliant in diagnosis of the many-sided sickness of mankind, but the cures elude us. "There's nothing wrong with modern man that the psychiatrist cannot exaggerate" is a quip that has an edge to it. For the consumption of pills and potions and pep-capsules is a symptom of an age living on its nerves, with no inward poise, or power to meet the time's demands. Shakespeare's memorable question:

> *Canst thou not minister to a mind diseased,*
> *Pluck from the memory a rooted sorrow,*
> *Raze out the written troubles of the brain*
> *And with some sweet oblivious antidote*
> *Cleanse the stuff'd bosom of that perilous stuff*
> *Which weighs upon the heart?*

still meets with only Shakespeare's answer —

> *Therein the patient*
> *Must minister to himself*

which to a sick soul is no answer at all.

Yet we need not minister to ourselves: there is a balm in Gilead, salvation is health, and by His stripes we can be healed.

The truth holds on three levels. The place of the *body* in the world's redemption must not be overlooked. In human flesh the atonement was wrought and by His death the body is redeemed: "He is the Saviour of the body". Thus beneath the cross we pray with confidence for His healing touch upon these frail and vulnerable bodies of ours, remembering always that *all* healing is divine healing; that His will for us in this as in all things, is our total good. If healing itself should be denied, yet pain can be transformed as, under the shadow of His Calvary, we discover in His hurt divine sympathy with our own.

So for the sickness of *sin*. "They that are whole have no need of the physician," Jesus had said, "but they that are sick. I came, not to call the righteous, but sinners." As He touched men's bodies, so did He touch with tenderness and power the blind, deaf, lame and paralysed, tortured and unclean *souls* of men to see the light and hear the truth and run, think, serve, and be clean. So does He still. But the touch is the touch of a pierced hand. He was wounded for our transgressions, and by His stripes we are healed.

But the truth goes deeper still. Jesus can bring healing to the deep, secret *wounds* so many carry in the soul, the legacy of long-past sin, the bitter fruit of suffering, or perhaps from cause unknown. There are hearts embittered and disillusioned, minds thwarted and repressed, at odds with themselves, spirits turned ever inwards who see and hear nothing beyond their own interest or comfort, or pride.

Some nurse to themselves a crippling sorrow; others, like Israel in Egypt, can listen to no Moses "for anguish of spirit and cruel bondage". Not a few seem permanently depressed, possessing no resilience of faith. Not a few feel constantly inferior, handicapped by their estimate of themselves. Not a few live persistently ill-adjusted lives, defeated by circumstance. And some fall into a chronically critical mood, that destroys all enjoyment, and appreciation.

Many, again, possess only a wistful faith, a dwindling hope, a fitful love, because the heart is sick and the soul bruised. And spiritual ill-health lies behind so much more: frustration and sadness in Christian service, difficulty and disappointment among Christian people, silence and reluctance when the soul should testify and sing.

Yet is not our Lord the Lord of *health*, infallible Physician of souls? Our modern faith is far too timid here, our insight far too shallow. Daringly, but deliberately, Paul links the disorders at the Lord's Supper, in the Church at Corinth, with the sickness prevalent amongst its members. Ought we to be surprised? Should not the memorial feast bring to us, often and again, the inward, continuing *healing* of the wounded spirit?

In the love of which the cross unfailingly assures us there is healing for all bitterness, all self-despair. In the pardon which the dying Lord pronounces there is healing for all shame and guilty fear. In the selflessness which on the cross confronts us there is healing for our morbid self-concern; in the call to love as He loves us there is powerful cure for the meanness of our hearts. The remembrance of what men did to Him makes our wounds smart the less, and in His claim to dispose of us as He thinks best — a claim which beneath the cross we cannot help conceding — there is balm for every disappointment and a cure for enviousness.

He is "the Lord who healeth us" — able to deal with every malady of soul that unfits us for His service, sets us against our fellows, or corrupts our joy. He has done it for many; He can do it for us.

O Saviour Christ, Thou too art Man;
* Thou hast been troubled, tempted, tried;*
Thy kind but searching glance can scan
* The very wounds that shame would hide;*

Thy word has still its ancient power
* No word from Thee can fruitless fall:*
Hear in this solemn evening hour
* And in Thy mercy heal us all.*

For by Thy stripes we are made whole.

5 The Timeless Hour

"This is your hour."
"He . . . obtained eternal redemption for us."
"One sacrifice for sins for ever . . . ."

Luke 22:53, Hebrews 9:12, 10:12

SOMEONE HAS INVITED us to consider what happens when a country lad, lying amid the heather on a summer night, gazes at the stars. Through the pupil of each eye, innumerable rays of light, that started their journey from distant corners of measureless space countless light-years ago, enter together, intersecting within the eye, and fall upon the retina. An inverted picture of the universe is reproduced upon a tiny patch of nervous network: the whole immensity of space focussed upon the infinitesimal membranes of the brain in the miracle of sight.

Barely credible with regard to *space*, such a narrowing down of vastness to the comprehension of the human mind becomes still more difficult to conceive with regard to *time*. The apocryphal *Book of James* attempts it. Speaking of the moment of Christ's birth, when Joseph has gone to seek help for Mary, the writer says: "Now I, Joseph, was walking, and I walked not. And I looked up to the air and saw the air in amazement, and I looked up into the pole of the heaven and saw it standing still, and the fowls of the heaven without motion. And I looked upon the earth, and saw a dish set and the workmen lying by it, and their hands were in the dish: and they that were chewing chewed not, and they that were lifting the food lifted it not, and they that put it to their mouth put it not thereto, but the faces of them all were looking upward. And behold there were sheep being driven, and they went not forward, but stood still; and the shepherd lifted his hand to smite them with his staff, and his hand remained up. And I looked upon the stream of the river and saw the mouths of the kids upon the water, and they drank not. And of a sudden, all things moved onward in their course".

So men felt about the birth of Jesus. Eternity was focussed in a moment, time stood still, and all divine and human history, intersecting, paused in an everlasting instant.

So men felt also, in the same degree, about the death of Christ. Stand with the first disciples beneath the cross, and you become aware of a growing feeling that time and eternity are somehow getting mixed together, that all history is being narrowed down to one hilltop, on one Friday, and, at the same time, that heaven lies about you. For they speak as men who saw eternity that afternoon.

That at least is the Biblical view of Calvary. The huge canvas of the Old Testament history, from the original purpose of the divine Creator, the making of the worlds, the multiplying of mankind and the rise of civilisation, through the settlement of races and the migrations of whole peoples to the rise and fall of vast Empires, is all a story of such narrowing down. Movement and progress, promise and hope are steadily focussed on one land, one Semitic race, one Hebrew people, one nation of Israel, one family of Abraham, one or two tribes of Judah and Benjamin, one family of David, and at long last One single splendid Son of David. Jesus. In the narrow compass of His thirty-three years, the whole preceding sacred history finds its meaning and fulfilment.

But the narrowing process continues. Three years of the thirty-three bear the main weight of divine purpose: beginning with the announcement, "The time is fulfilled", and continuing with the declaration, "Abraham rejoiced . . . kings, righteous men, prophets longed, to see this time". To Herod, Jesus sends the message, "Today and tomorrow . . . and the third day I am done". The urgency increases: "I must work the works of Him that sent me while it is day, for night cometh . . .". It intensifies still further: "What shall I say, Father save me from this hour? But for this cause came I unto this hour. . . . This is your hour! . . . A little while, and the world seeth me no more, for the things concerning me have an end". Then the decisive moment: "*Now* is the judgement of this world, *now* shall the prince of this world be judged". Three hours of darkness and the final cry, "It is accomplished!" close a whole epoch. Then the silent pause of death.

Then the canvas broadens out again, in widening circles of witness, in Jerusalem, Judea, Samaria, and to the uttermost parts of the world. A stream of new thought, inspiration, hope pours into history, lapping every shore, until out of every kindred and tongue and people and nation arise those who sing to the Lamb upon His throne the song of the redeemed.

Maybe it all sounds somewhat fanciful, but so the Bible sets the cross of Jesus in the perspective of all time as its focus and centre, the point to which all before leads up, prophecy, ritual and hope, and from which all afterwards derives its meaning. To New Testament thought the passion of Christ possesses this dramatic, time-shattering implication, that in it human history and God's eternity intersect: eternal issues hang on this event.

Christ is crucified by the determinate counsel and foreknowledge of God; the Lamb is slain from the foundation of the world. "No man taketh [my life] from me," says Jesus, "But I lay it down of myself. This commandment have I received of my Father." God *sent* His Son to be the propitiation for our sins. Paul, likewise, makes the whole process from glory through humiliation to the cross and back to glory, one long story of eternal atonement. Hebrews says, He obtained eternal redemption for us, by one sacrifice for sins for ever.

All through the story of the cross runs this haunting impression of things moving upon two levels at once. Jesus arranges for the earthly home of His mother, and promises to meet the dying thief in Paradise; He has hardly finished saying to the Father "Thy will be done", before He warns Pilate of the dire responsibilities he is incurring. Soon afterwards, Jesus is explaining, from Moses and the prophets, how these things had to be. The cross belongs to earth, and time and history, and the tragedy of human folly: no less it belongs to eternity and the infinite purposes of God.

It is easy to draw moral lessons from this dual aspect of the cross. To note, for example, how great issues may be worked out behind the apparent littleness of life. For Caiaphas, Pilate and the rest seem sometimes little men, bound by narrow horizons, moved by trivial motives, and wrangling over petty issues in a small subdivision of a long-fallen Empire. Yet to this day the spires lift the cross above our teeming cities! The passion of Jesus sets all human conduct in eternal perspectives.

So, too, one feels beneath the cross, as throughout the Bible, that the foreground of life is only understood when the background — the divine love, the ageless purpose, the eternal principles, the everlasting mercy — is kept in mind. The foreground obsesses us, but it can become pathetically shallow and unsatisfying without the background of God and of eternity.

Or we may remember the passing fashion of the world and the brevity of life. We all walk constantly on the graves of those who once were here; we are leasehold tenants of a crumbling house, and we shall pass, poor creatures of a day. But beneath the cross we hear another truth, that speaks of timeless love and life and hope. This is the great lesson Peter draws from the "everlasting event" of Calvary. "Ye were redeemed," he says, "from your *vain* manner of life", meaning amongst other things redemption from all that is frustrating, disappointing, barren, impermanent, corruptible, the vain and transient traditions of the world. Against all such futilities Peter sets the enduring gains of the redeemed, an undefiled, unfading, incorruptible inheritance, a crown of glory losing not its freshness, lives implanted by the incorruptible seed of the word of God, and the undimming ornament of a meek and quiet spirit.

By the death of Jesus, within the time-process but with eternal purpose, the status within the eternal scheme of those who believe is finally assured. Life, hope, security, inheritance within *that* realm are theirs, because He entered *this* realm of insecurity, change and loss, to die for them. Such eternal redemption is achieved, not with things themselves corruptible, like silver and gold, material things whose value varies in the markets of the changing world, but with the precious — permanently valuable — blood of Christ.

Only what abides is truly valued, and valid for eternity. Through the eternal Spirit He offered *Himself* unto God, by one offering perfecting for ever them that are sanctified. He redeems us from futility, and from time's destructive sway, because the price He pays is timeless, final and sufficient.

> *Dear dying Lamb! Thy precious blood*
> *Shall never lose its power,*
> *Till all the ransomed church of God*
> *Be saved, to sin no more.*

6 The Failure that Succeeds

"We trusted that it had been he which should have redeemed Israel."
"There they crucified him."

Luke 24:21, 23:33

WE SPEAK AFTER the manner of men. No one who stands for long beneath the cross of Jesus will have patience with discussion about the success or failure of His enterprise. It is the Lord's doing, and it is marvellous in our eyes.

And yet, the problem of handling failure is an urgent one for countless people, and touches very closely the nerve of Christian faith. For stark, relentless, crushing failure occasionally strikes our noblest schemes, our loftiest aspirations; and then perplexity and doubt can undermine our confidence and sap our resolution, may even leave us whipped and cynical, determined never again to attempt great things or set our hearts upon the peaks. If failure was due to intractable circumstance, we may come to feel embittered and unfairly used; if it was our own fault, it may be harder still to swallow, destroying all desire to try again.

And though it be "after the manner of men", the story of the cross has relevant things to say about failure. In one sense, the Easter glory hides from us the facts that weighed so heavily on the disciples while Jesus lay within the tomb. To them the failure, defeat, despair were all too real. Had there not been talk of feasts, and treasure, thrones, glory, power and a kingdom? Had they not argued precedence amongst themselves, and witnessed with a mounting hope His challenge to the city? They had felt the air thrill with Messianic excitement, and knew that they stood on the edge of momentous things.

"And they crucified him." No words could express more clearly the sudden change of mood, the sad realisation of disastrous facts, than those of the two walking to Emmaus: "We trusted it had been he which should have redeemed Israel". They had had good reason for their trust. But they had seen high expectations crash into stunning disillusion, all the exciting possibilities of that ride into Jerusalem fade into sudden and bewildering defeat. Jesus

31

had challenged, and had received His answer. He had dared, and failed. He had warned, pleaded, wept — and died in shame. Success had gone to Caiaphas. For weeks the High Priest had argued, plotted, bribed, astutely and with foresight, to get rid of Jesus, in spite of Roman law and popular feeling. And dramatically, completely, had he fulfilled his purpose, in the midst of Passover, with the help of those same crowds, under the very nose and by the hand of Pilate. Jesus had flung Himself against the conscience of His nation, had failed to waken it, and had perished. Caiaphas had led cynical and ruthless diplomacy to overwhelming triumph. And they who had hoped, shut themselves behind closed doors, or walked homewards and were sad.

Then Jesus stood again amongst them: and the moral universe turned over. All insights had to be revised, all judgments reversed. Failure was success, success a dismal, dangerous failure; defeat spelt victory and sorrow and darkness was the outer edge of glory. In the gloom of Calvary, and the brightness of Easter, what is failure? what is success? When Jesus fails successfully and Caiaphas succeeds disastrously, what shall we say?

The implications are simple and practical, but they can matter much to those who have attempted fine things and failed: maybe even more to those who count themselves successful.

Clearly, there is a success which is failure in disguise. Such was the triumph of Caiaphas, and instances may come to mind of others betrayed by similar success to their own undoing. Some succeed at too high a price for conscience; some to lose all charm, humility, and lovableness; some to be alienated from all they loved. Success may breed a self-destroying snobbery that isolates the soul in its little mirrored world. It can come between a spirit and its Lord, spoil all appetite for faith and worship and the things of God, and leave the heart disarmed and naked to temptation when it least expects assault.

Some climb on Christian reputation to material prosperity, and kick away the ladder at the last to show their worldliness of soul. And sometimes the path upward is strewn with those who have been overridden, brushed aside, ruthlessly used and then discarded, friendships sacrificed and even closer ties wilfully ignored in the mad scramble that makes money and unmakes the soul.

And what is it in the end but failure? The story of the rich fool — grown rich in legitimate ways, and in rewarding toil, yet a "fool" because bankrupt in soul and naked for eternity — is told a thousand times in Christian biography. Success like that of Caiaphas can be disastrous, both for the successful and for those who are dragged by it to ruin, as was Israel. Bitter indeed is the fruit of successful wrong!

Equally clearly, there is success which is achieved within sore failure. The victory of Jesus began within Gethsemane, gained strength throughout the trials, was consummated on the cross. He died unbroken, undefeated, commending His spirit to the Father in unshaken peace and dying with unclouded faith. That *is* triumph.

If we cannot see this, we must write off many lives as failures because they did not *see* their dreams fulfilled, their hopes accomplished. The writer to the Hebrews lists the great men of the past, their high expectations, their towering hopes, their noble confidence, and has to write of them all "these all died . . . not having received the promises". Are they then failures after all? "These died," he says, "in faith" — that was their victory.

To be found when the storm of doubt is past, still humbly trusting Christ, though chastened and subdued — that is victory. To find, when the fires of fierce temptation have scorched your soul that your song is muted, and your pride is gone, but faith remains — that is success. To know, when the assaults of pain have ended and the querulous, distressful mood has passed, that "thy faith fails not" — that is overcoming. To know after the heartbreak of sore failure, when all your work and prayer and striving prove of no avail, and your effort is rejected, your service unrewarded, that still you believe God, and will go on with Him: that is to be unbeaten, in the end.

To keep the vision, through the tears; to maintain the fight, despite the wounds; to go on running in the race, though falls are frequent; to maintain integrity and renew the drooping faith in spite of heartache and despondency: this is the true success of Christian souls. If more is given, thank God for it; but if this be the way you have to go, let not the enemy call it failure: it is to keep the faith, fight the good fight, and — God promises — to finish the course. And that is true success.

Clearly, once more, there is a failure which is but success in delay. Columbus never found his way to India. Nor did Carey find the South Sea islands, or Barnardo get to China. St. Joan did not live to see her France set wholly free. Who shall say such souls died in failure? Francis Thompson saw wretchedness and shame, a brief respite for creative work and early death, but his magic poetry forbids the cruel judgement men might pass on him. Perhaps no one, in the larger things of life, has shown the quality that is in him until he has wrested victory from defeat, fighting his way out of failure to courageous new beginnings.

John Mark, turning his back upon the earliest missionary enterprise, letting down companions and the cause, earned Paul's strong rebuke, but found the way to redeem his failure and regain his name. Peter learned the same humiliating road to finer fitness for the task among the lambs. Indeed, most of the disciple band had taste of it, as Jesus came among them after a long night's fruitless toil and showed them how to do the task they should have understood so much better than He!

No failure needs to break a man, or to belittle him: acknowledged, and confessed, its lesson learned, and put to use, it can remake him. This surely is the central message of the cross: the possibility, in God's mercy, of reassessment, re-equipment, recommissioning, for all who fail and fall. God has done glorious things with those whom — at some time in their career — the world would discount as useless and defeated: Jacob, and Moses, David and Jeremiah, Peter and Mary Magdalene merely begin a long, long list of those who in their day were hopeless failures until grace redeemed them.

This is the proof, and measure, of Christ's wonderful *success*. He died, rejected, disowned, forsaken, in darkness, apparently deserted and defeated: by His death He has achieved in countless hearts all He set out to do. He has seen of the travail of His soul, and will be satisfied.

ACHIEVEMENTS THAT BELIE DEFEAT

The bearing of burdens
The coronation of pain
The resistance of wrong
The forgiveness of sins
The revelation of love
The transfiguration of death

7 The Bearing of Burdens

*"Bel boweth down, Nebo stoopeth; their idols are upon the beasts
. . . a burden to the weary beast . . . . Hearken unto me, O house
of Jacob, and all the remnant of the house of Israel, that have been
borne by me from their birth, that have been carried from the
womb; and even to old age I am he, and even to hoar hairs will
I carry you: I have made, and I will bear; yea, I will carry, and
will deliver."*
*"Surely he hath borne our griefs, and carried our sorrows. . . .
Jehovah hath laid on him the iniquity of us all."*
*"Bear ye one another's burdens, and so fulfil the law of Christ.
. . . Each man shall bear his own load."*

Isaiah 46:1, 3, 4; 53:4, 6, Galatians 6:2, 5 (ASV)

THE GREATEST MODERN painting of our Lord's crucifixion is Sal-
vador Dali's "Christ of St. John of the Cross". It represents the
crucifix suspended against a dense black sky above a blue Italian
lake, and tilted forwards so that you look upon the Saviour from
above. Our Lord's head is bowed, His face being hidden, and His
body strains forward and downward from the great timbers of the
cross.

A postcard reproduction evoked from two teenagers one outstanding impression — the massive shoulders, and muscled arms of
the Carpenter of Nazareth. Once noted, they seem to hold the
centre of the painting. Is this Dali's meaning, that the whole
weight of the sin and sorrow of the race meets on those mighty
shoulders, and bows that noble head — that Jesus died bearing the
burden of the world?

It may well be so. The ancients conceived the world laid on the
broad shoulders of the god Atlas: Dali has given us a Christian
counterpart. "He hath *borne* our griefs and *carried* our sorrows.
. . . The Lord hath *laid on him* the iniquity of us all."

Life is not all burdens, and religious faith does not assume it
is. But each life *has* its burdens, which none can measure save
he who carries it. For the young it is mostly the burden of learn-
ing, of coming to terms with the world and with the past.

For others it means work, to earn one's lodging in a teeming world and pay for the air one breathes — which might have been another man's. Manual labour oppresses some; the burden of responsibility is heavier upon others: responsibility for far-reaching decisions, or large undertakings, or tending the children — the boys and girls of another generation — as with all their wants and weaknesses they rise to adult life.

As experience grows the burdens multiply. Man is made upright, but he carries more than all his fellow creatures for he bears upon his mind and spirit the tasks and duties of a lifetime. For many, physical weakness or affliction is added to the load; or the unkindness of others, or the failure of those once trusted, lies like lead upon the heart. A difficult situation within the family, an undeserved legacy of evil, a moral weakness left by sin, a besetting temptation never wholly conquered — all can add to the burden to be borne.

Ahead of all is the burden of age; at the end the burden of man's mortality. Though life is not all a bearing of loads, not to possess one is to be a passenger, an idler, a ne'er-do-well. If you are not carrying one, now, be sure that someone, somewhere, is carrying it for you — yours as well as his own.

One thing the cross of Jesus suggests is that bearing your own burden is the primary obedience of faith. Our persistent temptation is to evade the immediate load, seeking some far-off greatness, or dreaming impossible things. We long for wings, though nothing is more certain than that we would take our unrest with us. We envy another's situation, we succumb to the deceitfulness of distance, we believe we would be better Christians in someone else's shoes, or if we had another's chance.

In truth, we would be still the same — discontented, self-pitying, and evading our duty! The burden appointed is the one at hand. "Let every man," wrote Paul to *slaves*, "wherein he is called, therein *abide*, with God." To want to run away is simply rebellion.

But Christian obedience is obedience of *faith*, and this is vividly recalled in the attitude of Jesus to the cross. For Christ accepted His burden as the Father's appointment: "This commandment have I received of my Father". But had not *Caiaphas* prepared the burden, and *Judas* indicated where to lay it, and *Pilate* bound it securely in place? Certainly: yet they "could have no power at all except it were given from above". The reaction of Jesus is neither resentment nor resignation but obedience in faith. No matter what has contributed to the burden, who bound it upon one's shoulders, it is still possible to believe that the Father knows, and to carry it bravely because you are carrying it for God.

Remembering the spirit of Jesus towards His own fearful load we can hardly help noticing a second thing: the attitude of Jesus to others in the stress of His own suffering. As the darkness gathers round Him and the burdens press more heavily upon His heart, He remains as mindful of the needs of those about Him as ever He has been in Galilee's peaceful villages among the seaside hills. He never becomes absorbed in His own crisis, nor preoccupied with His own pain.

Approaching Jerusalem, He weeps for its doom, though He weeps not for His own. He has words of sympathy for the mothers of Jerusalem even as He carries His cross to the place of execution. He is aware of the temptation, and remorse, of the erring Peter, and His glance of loving rebuke catches Peter's eye in the midst of His own cross-examination. In the garden of betrayal He speaks swiftly to defend His friends even while His own hands are taken, and He heals the ear of Malchus ere they are bound. He has warning for Pilate, and care for John, love for His mother and grace for the dying thief, a prayer for those who crucify Him and His final thought is of the Father — all this as the burden of a whole world's grief and shame bore down upon His own heart.

This is the law of Christ, of which Paul speaks. To bear another's burden is to halve your own. Indian carriers, having only one package to carry, will nevertheless set the bamboo across their shoulders, with parcel one end and a stone the other, for balanced burdens are lighter to bear. This too the cross would say to heavy-laden souls.

Nevertheless we are not yet at the heart of the matter. The *central* thought is of Christ Himself, the Bearer of *our* burdens. "He bore *our* sins. . . . He taketh up and beareth away the sins of the world. . . . He hath borne *our* griefs and carried *our* sorrows. . . . The Lord hath laid on him the iniquity of *us all*." Jesus criticised the Pharisees for increasing men's burdens while not lifting a finger to help in the carrying. Calvary reveals the depth of His rebuke.

Of course, some part of the burden we must bear, to prove our manhood, test our worth, and take our share in the work of the world. But the burdens that crush are those we ought never to have taken up, because they are wrong, and wilful, and full of judgement. These He declares He has borne for us, and the rest He offers to share.

Isaiah's scathing picture is relevant here, because it lifts the whole meaning to timeless levels. Nebo and Bel were enormous Babylonian idols, carried in sacred procession on the backs of mules and oxen that staggered beneath the weight — "baggage bales for the backs of weary beasts". Not so have I dealt with you, says God to Israel: "I have made, and I will bear; even to hoar hairs will I bear *you*, and even to old age will *I* carry *you*". Irreligion, and false religion, add to the burdens men must struggle with: true faith lightens the load and God carries the carrier!

At Calvary we are permitted to see Him doing it. Many are the souls who, like Bunyan's pilgrim, have felt the thongs loosen and the burden fall at the foot of that cross.

> *And ye, beneath life's crushing load*
> *Whose forms are bending low,*
> *Who toil along the climbing way,*
> *With painful steps and slow,*
> *Look up! for glad and golden hours*
> *Come swiftly on the wing:*
> *Oh, rest beside the weary road,*
> *And hear the angels sing.*

"I have made, and I will bear," saith the Lord. "Come unto me all ye that labour and are heavy laden, and I will give you rest. . . . Cast thy burden upon the Lord," and though you cannot be relieved of all of it, yet "he shall sustain *thee*".

"For the Lord hath *laid on him* the iniquity of us all."

8 The Coronation of Pain

"Pilate therefore took Jesus, and scourged him. And the soldiers platted a crown of thorns, and put it on his head."
"Behold, and see if there be any sorrow like unto my sorrow."

John 19:1, 2, Lamentations 1:12

IT IS A CURIOUS fact that among all living things man appears to possess the highest capacity for suffering. The higher creatures stand in the scale of life, the wider and deeper their susceptibility to pain; the more developed their nervous system, the greater their sensitiveness to want and agony; the wider the range of experience, the more vulnerable to adversity. Man's power of imagination multiplies his suffering: and the sustained sadness of long-remembered sorrow is the price he pays for the gift of memory.

Man alone is troubled about his limitations, his creaturely dependence in a vast universe. Man alone knows moral suffering, the burden of guilt, the struggle for virtue, the cost of duty, the bitterness of failure. For man is reserved, in its fullness, the suffering of sympathy, the pain of bereavement, the long ache of loneliness. For human minds death too is intensified by mystery, contradiction, and religious overtones.

It is a melancholy distinction, but it marks the breadth and depth of human nature, and no philosophy or religion is worthy of attention unless it handles this fact honestly and adequately. It may bow before suffering, helplessly, as "the will of Allah". It may attempt to think itself into a world beyond both joy and pain. It may affect to despise it, cultivating a rigid self-discipline that admits neither pain nor sympathy. It may even seek to explain it away as a psychological illusion. All these reactions have been tried, and inadequate as they are, at least they shame the shallow hedonist, who persuades himself that life is made for pleasure, buries his head in entertainment, grows callous towards others' pain, and bitter with self-pity if adversity comes his way.

For suffering is *there*, a part of human life. The Christian faith accepts the fact: thorns beset mortal feet and wound sore the human spirit. Christianity assumes the truth within the ancient

41

story of a garden and a sin, a divine design put out of joint by human wilfulness. It begins with the ground cursed for man's fault, the nettle and the briar springing in Eden not because God willed it so but because man *must* learn the heinousness of sin.

The gospel begins with the thorns in the garden: but look where it ends! With One who (to borrow an apt phrase from J. S. Stewart) "took the thorns", woven by cruel hands into a mocking wreath, "and wore them as a crown". He bore our griefs and carried our sorrows, but by the way He bore them, by His own reaction to them, by the faith in which He met them, He transformed the symbol of suffering into a chaplet of glorious personal triumph.

Let there be no misunderstanding, the suffering was not symbolic but real, and complete. Every thorn was there: physical agony, mental distress, the dread of death, the sorrow of betrayal; the loneliness, ingratitude, disloyalty, false accusation, and injustice that hurt so deeply; the pain of seeing others weep for Him, and deliberate, mocking cruelty. All this He suffered, *plus* the hiding of the Father's face that the debt of sin might be fully paid —

> *Desperate tides of the whole great world's anguish*
> *Forced thro' the channels of a single heart.*

And yet His perfection shines through. No angry recrimination, no torturing self-pity, no whimpering for mercy, breaks from His lips. A Stoic centurion marvels at His endurance; love, forgiveness, gentleness, thought for others, courage, faith, sacrifice, every noble quality of the human spirit is here raised to the zenith of its power by the pain against which its beauty shines. This is one way the thorns become a crown, by being woven into the diadem of a refined and splendid soul.

Explain it how we may, a world without suffering would be a world without much that we admire. Without hardship, there could be no heroism; without pain, no patience; without adversity, no courage. The grandest music, the loftiest thought, the noblest literature, the saintliest devotion are all related somehow to man's suffering and struggle. Some other sort of world may be conceivable, but as things are, thorns crown the beauty of the best no less surely than they embitter the selfish and shallow heart.

As with character, so with faith. Jesus made the thorns a crown by showing that in the deepest darkness God is still at hand. For many, suffering is intensified by perplexity. Pain can obscure the face of God, and doubt feed on adversity to impugn the love or wisdom of our Father. God seems far away; we imagine Him angry, or indifferent to us.

Yet beneath the cross of Jesus we learn otherwise. Even in the mysterious crisis of atonement, Jesus can still speak of "My God, *my* God . . .". When the final moment comes, it is "Father, into thy hands. . .". And in all the previous hints and warnings of rejection, pain and death, there is never a doubt that the Father's way is best, and the Father's purpose only good.

> *Is there a tear He did not shed,*
> *A pain He did not know,*
> *A burden sore He never bore,*
> *Some wholly private woe?*
> *None — yet in darkness light abides,*
> *And in His anguish, peace:*
> *He knew God's love His pain above*
> *And in faith found release.*

And so the saints find, too. What else mean the testimonies every minister hears? In the hour I dreaded, courage 'came'." "By the time I had to decide, my mind was calm and clear." "I do not know why, but I've always dreaded death, and now I don't. I'm going home, and I do not mind. Everything is all right." And when the crisis is past, the operation over, the fear removed, we feel a little foolish, we wonder why we were afraid, and can only thank God for undeserved and unexpected grace.

This is the inner victory of faith, learned at the cross, and such trust is the crown of piety. It finds in the darkness a supporting hand; beneath the fall, the everlasting arms, and knows

> *The clouds may veil the sun, and tears my eyes,*
> *Still reigns my Lord beyond these curtained skies.*

Once more, and yet more wondrously, Jesus made the thorns of life a crown by somehow lifting the whole dread fact of human suffering to a new level — that of sacrifice. He took the things men did to Him, and *used* them for His purposes. Accepting what He might have so resented, He not only defeated those who reviled Him, He wrested the weapon from their hands and made it His lever to uplift the world. Their very thorns become the coronet by which His regal claim is recognised; their cross of hate, His throne of love; the nail-prints and the scourge-scars and the spear-thrust, so many badges of His valour kindling loyalty in His men. All is sublimated, changed, transformed to redemptive purposes, by the way He bore it.

The crown of thorns was no essential part of the atonement, but the cruel invention of a callous soldier with a twisted sense of humour and a flair for mockery: yet Jesus redeemed the ugly thing by the beauty of His spirit. A dedicated heart can consecrate any experience to positive ends. Whatever men, or life, may do to us can be lifted in pierced hands to God in sacrifice, an avenue of testimony, a discipline of faith, an act of simple obedience and submission, a means of spiritual refinement. Through it men may come to know our God a little better by the grace He gives to us, by the reflection of His Spirit through our pain.

These insights, doubtless, are familiar truths to Christian hearts — the enhancement of character through adversity, the refinement of faith through suffering, the positive value discoverable in every experience. But what is obvious to minds taught in the school of the Crucified is really a new thing in the earth, an achievement of the cross. Pagan suffering is a cruel, soul-poisoning bitterness. Only when one has pondered long the passion of our Lord, and found life through His death, can one really understand how Matheson, blind, disappointed, lonely, could find grace to sing —

> I may not cast Thy cross away;
>   Thou gavest me Thy yoke to share;
>   Give but the arm new nerve each day,
>   Give but the heart fresh love to bear —
> Until my thorn become my flower,
>   Till death itself in life shall rise,
>   And human sorrow's midnight hour
>   Ring the first chimes of Paradise.

9　The Resistance of Wrong

"He that hath no sword, let him sell his garment, and buy one."
"Put up . . . thy sword."

Luke 22:36, Matthew 26:52

THE NEW TESTAMENT is full of the martial spirit. The clash
of armour, weapons, fighting, battle, the shout of victory, sound
through its pages. The cross, in apostolic thought, becomes the
symbol of — amid so many things — Christ's strenuous resistance
against wrong.

Hearts acutely sensitive to the horrors of modern warfare are
sometimes genuinely uneasy about the use of military metaphors
in religion. Others of us dislike the language because we have
furled our banners, sheathed our swords, doffed our armour, and
bade the trumpeters be quiet, have shaken hands with the King's
enemies and adopted a most immoral pacificism towards things we
ought vigorously to oppose.

Literary tastes apart, we certainly cannot follow Christ while
claiming exemption from the good fight of faith. All through our
Lord's ministry a storm of conflicting forces is gathering about
His head. From the temptation in the wilderness, and the clash
with the Pharisees, to the threats of the Sanhedrin and the confronting of Pilate, divergent currents meet and break upon Jesus.
In the final hours He speaks of "overcoming", explains to the
Governor the warfare in which His servants would fight, tells
the disciples of the imminent challenge of "the prince of this
world".

Afterwards, the theme of *Christus Victor* fills the minds of
the first evangelists. Death is swallowed up in *victory*; He has
ascended up on high leading many *captives*; He expects His
enemies to become His footstool; He *made spoil* of principalities
and powers, *triumphing* over them in His cross; He *overcame*,
and leads us in the train of His *triumph*, more than conquerors
through Him that loved us.

This is the abiding truth beneath the soldierly metaphors:
Christ did battle in our name against all that threatened our

peace, and we are enlisted in that war, to share His conflict and to inherit His victory. If, in spite of all the martial hymns, the idea is strange and obscure to us, it is because Christ deliberately rejected all the weapons with which we would naturally fight, and the strategy we would most readily follow, choosing instead to submit and to suffer. This we feel — in our heart of hearts — is wonderful, but it is not war.

Peter, in the garden, flashed the sword in Christ's defence, but Jesus would have none of it. Into His mind slips the possibility of praying for twelve legions of angels, but the possibility is at once rejected: there must be no spectacular display of superior force. As His kingdom is not of this world, so the weapons of this conflict are not carnal but spiritual: yet the war is on, and strongholds are pulled down.

To assess the struggle we must look deeper. In the passion of Jesus great forces wrestle for the soul of the world, forces which divide between them the control of history. On one side stands the love of power, the wish to dominate; on the other, readiness to wash men's feet. Pride of race, religion and privilege are ranged against humility and self-abasement. Passionate prejudice, prepared to misuse all forms of law and descend to ruthless violence, confronts a meek and gentle heart. Calculating ambition, cynically sacrificing the innocent to save itself, is matched against the utter selflessness of Jesus.

An ancient religion, consciously upon the defensive, lacking inspiration, clinging by hypocrisy, half-truth and ritual to the vestiges of power, confronts in Jesus simplicity, truth, authority, the Spirit of the living God. Christ the healer, teacher, friend of sinners, Jesus of the donkey and the tears, faces Caiaphas, Judas, Pilate, the mob, the pride of Jewry, the power of Rome, and all the innate selfishness of human hearts: His only armour truth and gentleness, kind words and simplicity, healing and forgiveness!

Yet this is war. Jesus rejects our weapons, but He will not withdraw from the fight. He is in the thick of it. His heart is the arena, His cross the battlefield, His own life the gauntlet He flings down before the hosts of evil.

O love of God! O sin of man!
In this dread act your strength is tried.
And victory remains with love,
For He, our Lord, is crucified.

Faber is so *right*. Too often we imagine that victory might have lain in somehow evading the end, outwitting the enemy, meeting spite, force, hatred, lies, with mightier and more terrible weapons, "with the breath of His mouth slaying the wicked". We fail to see that that would be descending to the enemy's level, entire capitulation and defeat.

Sometimes we speak as though all victory lay in resurrection: but still greater triumph lay in His regal and unforced submission. Not all the worst that earth or hell could do sufficed to turn Him from His purpose. Nothing could embitter for a moment that loving heart, or arouse a second's weakening self-pity, or make Him trim a word, abate a claim, pray for revenge, or call on God for vindication. To the bitterest end, gentleness, simplicity, humility, truth persist, undefeated, and undismayed. Jewry, Rome, the sin of all humanity, have had their finest chance, and utterly failed to break Him. The prince of this world finds neither weakness nor foothold in His nature. Victory remains with love *because* Jesus our Lord is crucified.

Thus beneath the cross of Jesus thousands have learned the nature of the spiritual conflict, the strategy involved, and the meaning of victory. It is not enough to say that truth will conquer without our aid; he that hath no sword must sell his garment and buy one — or perhaps go back to that place of spiritual betrayal where once he threw it from him. He that has no stomach for the fight, had better examine again the terms of his enlistment: the gentle Jesus needs no cowards. Light struggles with darkness, love with hatred, lies with truth, the word of God against the contradictions of men; the treatment of the world, the temptations of the world, the prince of the world, all are to be overcome — or Christ must be betrayed again.

How then can we fight? What strategy is worthy of the cross and fitting to the spirit of the Christ? The basis of His strategy lay in *keeping His own hands clean*. "This man hath done nothing amiss. . . . they sought to accuse . . . and found none . . . . I betrayed innocent blood." In Him that generation saw One Man walk the mire unstained, One Man resist and overcome. He set against the drift of things one pure, victorious soul, and that is the first and greatest thing that any can do: without pride, or condemnation, or contempt, to keep our own hearts clean.

The method of His strategy lies in *fearless challenge* and forthright attack. At the center of the Jewish world He delivers His fivefold hammer-blow upon the nation's conscience — the raising of Lazarus, the ride into the city, the "cursing" of the figtree, the cleansing of the Temple, the exposition of the vineyard parable of Isaiah. Each is a significant and telling comment upon the situation in the Jewish state and church: and the weapon is truth, spoken with authority, demonstrating life and power. Here is no passive resistance to evil: they had to silence Him or submit. Too often we need merely be ignored!

The background of His strategy is His *silence for Himself.* Vocal for others, forthright for the truth, He yet stands barely speaking — and never more than the direct and minimum truth — before Caiaphas, Herod, and Pilate. The essential questions answered, He pleads, argues, protests nothing for His own cause. Where all too often we are demanding fairness, urging our deserts, loudly protesting our rights and our injustice — till the world cannot distinguish our self-seeking from our cause — He stands mute and uncomplaining. And His way wins.

The crown of His strategy is the hardest point of all: it lies in His *meek acceptance* of the cost of godliness, the price of truth. This is a world where the good man pays for being good, where he who would resist evil must reckon with a Calvary, with loneliness and loss and pain and disappointment, and not grow cynical or bitter or resentful. Only so can evil be exposed and the hearts of men awakened — as we too bear the cross He bore.

But so we share His victory; indeed, this *is* victory. Not to be brought low, and overcome of evil, but to overcome evil with good; not to be separated from the love of Christ, but to be found when the battle is done still at His side; not to lose faith, but in the darkness and the strife to hold fast. This is resistance; this is triumph. Starting beneath the cross He leads us in the train of His triumph, more than conquerors through Him that loved us.

10 The Forgiveness of Sins

"Father, forgive them."
"Whether is it easier to say. . . , Thy sins be forgiven thee. . .?"
"God for Christ's sake hath forgiven you."

Luke 23:34, Mark 2:9, Ephesians 4:32

AT ALMESBURY ABBY Queen Guinevere did penance for her intrigue with Sir Lancelot, against the king. To her at length came Arthur, grief-stricken and alone, wronged and dishonoured, yet unwilling to die unreconciled. Whether in all the melodious magic of the *Idylls of the King* Tennyson does justice to the subsequent scene, is a nice question. Arthur makes an interminable speech, full of reproach, rehearsing the dire effects of the Queen's treachery. He will not contemplate reunion, though he speaks of loving still:

> *Yet think not that I come to urge thy crimes,*
> *I did not come to curse thee, Guinevere,*
> *The wrath . . .*
> *. . . is past*
> *And all is past, the sin is sinned, and I,*
> *Lo! I forgive thee as Eternal God*
> *Forgives. . . .*
> *But hither shall I never come again.*

One hundred and fifty lines of Tennysonian eloquence to get done what moderns would accomplish with a cocktail and a kiss! And is forgiveness given in the end? The past remains unaltered, the act is still condemned, the consequence continues to be borne: what then *is* forgiveness?

The answer we make reveals what depth of moral insight we possess. A shallow thoughtlessness takes forgiveness entirely for granted, an obvious, simple, easy thing. But it is neither.

> *The moving finger writes, and having writ*
> *Moves on: nor all thy piety nor wit,*
> *Can lure it back to cancel half a line,*
> *Nor all thy tears wash out a word of it.*

Is, then, forgiveness possible?

Or is it simple? The words of Jesus at Capernaum suggest a truth beside the one intended — "Whether is *easier*, to say . . . forgive. . . ?" There is something difficult, complex, miraculous, in every act of pardon.

Nor is it cheap. It is not easy to be gracious when parents meet again the drunken driver who destroyed their child; or when a father confronts the libertine who dishonoured a well-loved daughter; or when one partner of a happy marriage helplessly watches the other, enticed, deceiving and unfaithful. What, *then*, is the cost of mercy, and of self-control?

Clearly there are questions here that call for careful answer.

(1) Where hearts are big enough, and love is deep, forgiveness is certainly possible. People of goodwill, aware of their own frailties, can easily agree to let the past be past. But can God forgive — God the all-holy, the judge of men?

The Gospel declares He can. To the palsied, Jesus said, "Thy sins be forgiven thee"; to a woman of the streets, "Go in peace, thy sins are forgiven"; to another, "Neither do I condemn thee; go, and sin no more". One who pleads, "God, be merciful to me, a sinner," is declared to be "justified". Christ's blood is shed, His death is to be "preached" — "for remission of sins": He prays upon the cross, "Father, forgive them . . ."; He came "to give his life a ransom for many".

Forgiveness fills the gospel, and finds a score of metaphors. It is the father's welcome to the prodigal, the carrying homeward of the sheep that was lost. It is the eating and drinking of the Son of God with sinners. It is the kiss upon the traitor's brow, the tender look across the courtyard at the erring Peter, the strong promise spoken to the dying thief.

Forgiveness is the healing touch of the Physician for the sick in soul; it is a cancelling of debt when we have naught to pay. It brings cleansing to defilement, comfort to despair, renewal of opportunity to those who have lost heart.

Forgiveness enters court with verdict of acquittal — saying, with Stephen, "Lord, lay not this sin to their charge"; then we call it justification. Forgiveness climbs the altar steps to offer sacrifice, making "satisfaction" for sin — then we call it expiation. Forgiveness treads the market place to ransom the enslaved — here it is called redemption. It brings together in friendship hearts long estranged by wrong, and we name it reconciliation. It cancels obligations once incurred but now too great to be discharged: we call it then "remission".

In every guise, divine forgiveness is the centre of the Church's thinking, the burden of her message. Paul and Augustine, Luther and Bunyan, Wesley, Booth, Moody and Graham — all her leaders are forgiven men preaching forgiveness with forgiving power. Forgiveness *is* the gospel, and countless hearts can prove its saving truth.

(2) Granted then its possibility, what does forgiveness mean? It cannot be mere carelessness condoning wrong. Nor moral weakness lightly excusing punishment. Nor is it just pretending to forget, or balancing evil done with goodness claimed — or promised. What's done is done, and must remain, unchanged.

Yet *the sinner* is changed. The thief pleads, "Lord, remember me!" A woman of the city weeps over Jesus' feet, the prodigal trudges homewards, the publican prays for mercy. Blunted conscience is made sharp again, inflamed desire is disciplined, the hardened heart is humanised, the weakened will made strong. Sorrow for sin done, shame at its remembrance, restitution of its harm, and abandonment of its ways, all follow from the experience of pardon. Few things work so radical a change as moral conviction followed by forgiveness. And *relationships* are changed. In our deepest penitence, it is not the fear of hell that shakes us — else are we frightened and not contrite. It is not the dread of punishment — else are we only remorseful; it is not merely the sense of shame. Always, in the end, within our penitence is the tormenting sense of being out of touch with God, beyond the reach of love, self-banished from His interest, unfitted for His presence. Such sense of alienation from the source of love and life, lies at the root of a true sense of sin and is the deepest need forgiveness has to meet. To know oneself reconciled — received back, accepted, at the Father's side, "friends again" in fellowship — is to feel forgiven.

The *situation*, too, is changed. How the bitterness of heart is sweetened, the self-reproach lifted from the soul! Shame can become the spur to stedfastness. Social condemnation, acknowledged now, can become the means to make reform more humble and reliable. Experience of sin's consequence can make for wisdom, and for zeal. Punishment accepted can be the discipline that redeems. What a depth of consecration the memory of dying Stephen wrought in Saul of Tarsus! By the miracle of divine forgiveness even mistakes and failures are made to yield some positive good in the total pattern of our lives.

All this change is central to the meaning of forgiveness. So, too, is the divine entrustment which forgiveness brings. In every act of pardon there is commissioning to new tasks: David to "teach transgressors Thy ways"; Isaiah hears, "Whom shall I send, and who will go for us?" The woman forgiven adultery is told to "go and sin no more", Peter to "feed my sheep". Paul is "a chosen vessel unto me". This is no coincidence. God, forgiving us, believes in us, in our ability (with grace) to stand where we had fallen, to conquer where we were defeated. Forgiveness is always an enabling new start; God takes us again into service, assigns us work to do within His kingdom. His pardon makes us feel that we are valued, wanted, trusted. That is the fullness of its meaning, and the foundation of its joy.

(3) What, finally, of its cost? Here perhaps our modern thought is shallowest. Often, ourselves, resentful and unforgiving we lightly assume that others should find forgiveness easy. We have even imagined a kind and gentlemanly God, "only too" willing to forgive and forget!

But this is childish. Ill would it fare with us if God cared as little for justice as we sometimes do! Evil is evil: to forgive is rarely easy, never cheap — and the cross of Jesus is the measure of its cost to God. God "spared not his own Son"; we are "forgiven for Christ's sake". We have "redemption, even the forgiveness of sins, through his blood". The question of the risen Lord remains to humble us: "Ought not the Christ to have suffered these things?" and His answer to reassure us: "Thus it behoved Christ to suffer . . . that repentance and remission of sins should be preached in his name". There was no other way.

That is why forgiveness is possible — and free. Why, too, countless thousands of believers have sung the song of the redeemed. They have found, with Bunyan's pilgrim, that before the cross the burden slipped from their back and was lost to view in the mouth of His grave.

And that is why, forgiveness being so costly, it binds the forgiven soul in endless love and gratitude to the Forgiver. They love most, who most have been forgiven. And all truly Christian devotion is the life-service of forgiven hearts, unpayably indebted for a priceless boon. 2-8-78

> *For you and for me*
> *He prayed on the tree:*
> *The prayer is accepted, the sinner is free.*
> *The sinner am I,*
> *Who on Jesus rely,*
> *And come for the pardon God will not deny.*

11 The Revelation of Love

"The Father himself loveth you."
"Herein is love, not that we loved God, but that he loved us, and sent his Son to be the propitiation for our sins."
"God commendeth his love toward us, in that . . . Christ died for us."

John 16:27, I John 4:10, Romans 5:8

> *Inscribed upon the cross we see*
> *In shining letters, God is love.*

IT IS GREATLY to be feared that we have sung, or heard, that statement so often that we are no longer capable of being surprised at it; indeed, we are hardly aware of what it says. We are so acquainted with the thought that the cross of Jesus proves the love of God that we miss altogether the astonishing, blazing paradox of pointing to His nailprints and saying, "Look, that shows that God is kind!"

We cry with Pilate, Behold the Man, bound, bleeding and hounded to death, and we declare with ecstasy, that is how much God loves us; we tell of an innocent Man shamefully treated, and bid men therefore to believe that the King of the world is just and good and true, "standing within the shadows keeping watch above His own". All that the world sees is just one more stark tragedy of injustice and betrayal; and the average mind, if it would relate the story to God at all, shares the reaction of the small girl: "I think God was cruel to let Jesus die".

That Jesus taught the love of the Father for His children, bidding us take note of the clothing of the lilies, the impartial gifts of sun and rain, the sureness of the harvest, and the certainty of the kingdom, is not in question. But the cross seems rather to destroy the argument than to clinch it: Christ's death appears the final contradiction of His faith.

Yet those who stood nearest to the event did not see it so. They declare that "God commended his own love toward us, in that while we were yet sinners Christ died for us". "Herein is love, not that we loved God but that he loved us, and sent his Son to be the propitiation for our sins." "He that spared not his own Son, but delivered him up for us all, how shall he not with him also freely give us all things?" "God so loved the world that he gave his only begotten Son. . . ."

With the reasons for this difference of viewpoint we are not here concerned. Certainly the first Christians entertained no idea that it took Calvary to make God love the world! They probably felt more deeply than we usually do, the *unity* between Christ and God — that "God was in Christ, reconciling the world unto himself" and by Christ's death commending His own love towards men. They spoke, too, more of the giving of God, even to the ultimate gift of an only Son, and God's "not sparing" His Son, thus striving to express the sense of what redemption cost the heart of God. As for "letting Jesus die", the first believers would say it was Jesus or the race, and the fault of that lay wholly with men; the way out of the dilemma was a compact of divine love between Father and Son which involved the cross to save mankind.

But explanations aside, of this they were confident: the love of God was revealed at Calvary as it was revealed nowhere else in nature, history or in man's experience. And that is deeply significant.

It scarcely needs saying that the divine love seen at Calvary is love *in disguise*. The love of God is not linked to the death of Jesus, in the New Testament, before it happened, but only afterwards, as men reflected upon its effects and entered into the salvation Christ had wrought. Then its appalling cost, and the wonder of the grace that planned, the love that carried through so glorious a scheme, broke upon their hearts. But these were after-thoughts, the fruit of deeper insight and more intimate experience of God.

It is a commonplace of Christian piety that God does not work in ways obvious to finite minds. He is His own interpreter, and impatience learns no secrets. Cowper's familiar descriptions of God's providence, as dark clouds big with blessings, a frown that hides a smile, buds that are bitter but breaking into fragrance, are true to all we know of the faithful Father's dealings with His children.

> *Is my gloom, after all,*
> *Shade of His hand, outstretched caressingly?*

It is: for the hiding of God's power is nothing to the veiling of His love in the disguise of hard days; but the love, like the power, is *there*, inexhaustible, unchanging, measureless and free.

In a deeper sense, too, the divine love seen at Calvary is love *amid darkness*. Just where most would say the love of God is in eclipse, there the New Testament declares it shines in noonday splendour. Perplexity and fear and doubt seem natural beneath the cross; but there men have found the comfort of undying love and the assurance of a daring faith.

This is why Christian hearts could shout that neither death nor life, things present nor things to come, could separate them from the love of God in Christ. They had read that love in tragedy, and nothing that could happen — tribulation, distress, persecution, peril — could challenge faith more strongly. Nothing *more* terrible, more painful, more unjust, could ever confront them than already they had seen. Yet in it they had found and felt the everlasting love, and seen the heart of God towards men. And reading God's tender compassion in the darkness of the cross, they could read it anywhere.

The third thing to be said brings us nearer to the centre of the truth: the divine love seen at Calvary is love *at its most downright*: it does not shirk our direst need, or spend itself in glowing poetry about life's rosier joys, but is set against the grim backcloth of our suffering and the fear of death. God has chosen to spell out His love to us in the language of sorrow, injustice, agony and death, and for that we can never be sufficiently grateful. One cannot point the blind to sunsets, or the deaf to song of birds; one cannot bid the lonely, desolate heart remember the joy of human friendship as evidence God loves: but one can point to Jesus, whatever the grief or fear or agony, and tell them of God's sympathy.

Divine love is realistic, honest, and strong; it meets us at our calvaries, and shares with us our pain.

> *Think not thou canst sigh a sigh*
> *And thy Maker is not by;*
> *Think not thou canst weep a tear,*
> *And thy Maker is not near.*

> *Oh! he gives to us his joy*
> *That our grief he may destroy;*
> *Till our grief is fled and gone*
> *He doth sit by us and moan.*

Only the passion of our Lord could ever have taught men that.

And then, of course, the very centre of the truth lies beyond even man's suffering, and poses the problem of man's sin. That the Creator cares for His handiwork, the Father for His child is not so wonderful: but what if the handiwork be marred, the child rebellious, ungrateful, wayward and wicked? What if men should say to the King, "We will not have this man to reign over us"? or of God's Son, "This is the heir, come let us kill him"? Will love hold then?

The dying Christ declares it does: "Father, forgive them. . .". This is the ultimate in loving, that God was in Christ reconciling to Himself a world ungrateful, alienated, guilty and forsworn. The divine love seen at Calvary is love at its divinest just because it is set against the foil of human sin, and seen in its redemptive power. God does not only love, He condescends to *commend* His love towards us, in that while we were yet sinners, Christ died for us. The Lord's arm is not shortened, nor the divine compassion limited by human merit:

> *Through all the depths of sin and loss*
> *There sinks the plummet of the cross;*
> *And never yet the depth was found*
> *Deeper than His cross can sound.*

And that is the final measure of the love revealed at Calvary.

> *So, the All-Great were the All-Loving too —*
> *So, through the thunder comes a human voice*
> *Saying, "O heart I made, a heart beats here!*
> *Face, my hands fashioned, see it in myself.*
> *Thou hast no power nor may'st conceive of mine,*
> *But love I gave thee, with myself to love,*
> *And thou must love me, who have died for thee!"*

12 The Transfiguration of Death

*"Verily I say unto thee, To day shalt thou be with me
in paradise."*
"O death, where is thy sting?"

Luke 23:43, I Corinthians 15:55

IT IS A BEWILDERING business trying to sort out the inconsistencies
of those who criticise the Christian faith. At one time, Christian
believers are represented as morbid pessimists, finding fault with
life and obsessed with thoughts of death, unhealthily fascinated
by the horrors of mortality. At another, they are caricatured as
foolish escapists, living in a faery world of wishful thinking, with
golden streets and pearly gates and angels and chariots coming
forth to carry them home; irresponsible optimists dodging reality!

When the former accusation is in fashion, much is made of
the interminable medieval sermons upon death, the sombre tone
of some devotional meditation, the death's-head at the feast and
the death-symbol in much decoration, and the more gruesome
passages in the poetry of Donne. Even so, one wonders if the
critics have weighed the appalling medieval mortality-rate, the
recurrent European plagues, the place death holds in Shakespeare's world. Where precisely does morbidity end and realism
begin?

When the other charge is made, about pie in the sky, it is the
extravagant attitude of some of the martyrs, the poor taste of some
funeral hymns and customs, the admitted shallowness of much
conventional consolation, that furnishes excuse. Christians might
be more impressed with this if the criticism did not come from
probably the most escapist generation in all history, wildly bent
upon emotional flight from frightening reality, frantically beating
out its pseudo-negroid rhythms, accelerating its pace, filling its
mind with trivial distractions, drugging its sensitivity with nar-
cotics, alcohol and bromides. And all, lest perchance it might hear
another H-bomb detonate, or glimpse above the neon-lights a glowing mushroom cloud.

He who in this age would charge the Christian faith with wish-

58

ful thinking, or with sentiment, is very ill-advised. Nothing could be more abominably sentimental than the attitude of the average blasé pagan towards death. The saccharine hypocrisies of the modern "mortician's" technique of painless bereavement and synthetic consolation beggar description. And the mawkish symbolism of deliberately un-Christian representations of death's meaning — the shattered column, the overturned wineglass, the broken lutestring, and the rest — like the shallow mock-stoicism that refuses to be comforted, preferring to rely on "a glass of something afterwards" and a very self-conscious stiff upper-lip, does not strike the average Christian as more intelligent, or more realistic, than the statements of the creed.

Christianity at any rate accepts the fact of death. When everything has been said about man's greatness, prowess, intellect, achievement, this still remains: he dies. Accepting it, the Christian faith reckons with mortality as the ultimate exposure of the worldly hope men set their hearts upon, the worthlessness of avarice, ambition, lust and pride. And so accepting death, and reckoning with it, Christianity has also wondrously transformed it, by daring to see beyond it everlasting life.

Hearts with humanity enough to feel the sorrows of their fellows do not despise any means of consolation. But far more is involved in the Christian hope than merely finding comfort in bereavement. The Christian thought of death sets life itself in true perspective. It makes all experience richer by the light of immortality, all decisions more significant for their immeasurable consequences, all struggle more worthwhile for its infinite reward.

Love is more enriching for its unbreakable endurance; duty is more demanding for its timeless authority; injustice, martyrdom, sacrifice are more tolerable for the certainty of vindication; pain, frustration, disappointment lose their power to crush when man lives forever. It is not escapist thus to make life more earnest, morality more imperative, death more meaningful. It is but spiritual insight into the dignity of man, the nature of the universe, the meaning of experience, and the heart of God.

All faiths and philosophies, of course, have in their measure sought to soften death. Christianity alone has dared to challenge death by means of death, to overcome the grave within the grave. This is the final, staggering paradox of Christian faith: it is on

Calvary that death itself is finally transfigured, and in Christ's tomb its sting is drawn.

"Our Saviour, Jesus Christ, hath abolished death, and brought life and immortality to light. . . . He was made a little lower than the angels, that he by the grace of God should taste death for every man. . . . He also himself partook of flesh and blood that through death he might destroy him that had the power of death, and deliver them who through fear of death were all their lifetime subject to bondage." "Blessed be God," says Peter, "who hath begotten us again unto a living hope by the resurrection of Jesus Christ from the dead." "Thanks be unto God," cries Paul, "who giveth us victory through our Lord Jesus Christ." "God has given us eternal life," declares John. "Because I live, ye shall live also" is the promise of Jesus.

Doubtless these utterances are superb statements of religious faith: but we miss their real significance unless we see them also as the convinced testimony of men for whom, in fact, death has been transformed. The speakers mean that for them this has already happened: the power of death to terrify is broken, the fear of death is gone, the bitterness of man's mortality is lifted from their hearts, death's sting is ended. Henceforth, "to live is Christ, to die is gain". With perfect sincerity men and women have learned of Jesus to face death with a cheer, to greet "gentle brother death, who comes to conduct us unto Christ," and praise God for "our sister, the death of the body, and her twin who is but sleep".

> O generous love, that He who smote
> In man, for man, the foe
> The double agony in man
> For man should undergo.
>
> And in the garden secretly
> And on the cross on high
> Should teach His brethren, and inspire
> To suffer and to die.

This then is the sober truth of the matter: Christ's death has transfigured death, and faith in Him has outfaced fear. Yet because the fear of death is mainly imaginative, it is not precise statements of the truth that help us most, but pictures and persuasive parables. Jesus gives us three.

One represents the after-life as *feasting* in God's presence. His table is spread, the guests assemble from all quarters of the globe, the new wine of the kingdom is poured, places are reserved. Harlots, sinners and aliens are invited to recline at table with the great ones of sacred story, the poor are carried to "Abraham's bosom" — the place next the greatest beside God's table. A picture of course, but set against the neglect and want of a wretchedly poor earthly life begging favours at the rich man's door, or seen as heaven's answer to earth's thousands of dispossessed, the picture yields its meaning. All the spirit's deepest hungers satisfied, all life's needs and longings perfectly fulfilled: such Jesus promises. For death is but a covered way to life's completeness.

Christ's second picture represents the after-life as *entrance upon a Temple-home*. "In my Father's house are many lodging places," and the phrase echoes words He spoke at twelve, and again at the cleansing of the Temple. Possibly thoughts of the home at Bethany are in His mind, the home where more than once He had found shelter, rest and peace; perhaps David's words were in His mind: "I will dwell in the house of the Lord for ever". Certainly Jesus meant that God's family must at last be gathered home, and where God is, is home and Temple all in one. There the heart shall find its rest, the soul its satisfaction, the conscience ease, the spirit worship. All we have wanted to be, we shall be — at home, in God.

And Christ's third picture is of a sheltered, park-like *garden*, protected from the violence of weather and wild beasts, a place prepared for relaxation and for deep enjoyment. "To-day shalt thou be with me in paradise." To the Hebrew mind, it was a recaptured garden, the long-lost bliss of Eden, regained in man's redemption, where once again man might walk in innocence, in company with God. From the Hebrew thought it passed with Jesus, into the Christian hope: "Him that overcometh I will give to eat of the tree of life which is in the midst of the paradise of God". To the dying brigand, his life now going out in violence and pain, Jesus promises rest and deep enjoyment in the place prepared for everlasting joy.

And truly, here is all we need to know. Beyond death there is *life*: "Thou shalt be . . . ". Beyond death there is *welcome*: "Thou, even thou, shalt be. . . ". Beyond death there is *Christ*: "Thou shalt be with me. . . ". Beyond death there is *joy and satisfaction*: "Thou shalt be with me in paradise". The words of dying men bespeak attention, these words above all others. For death has never been the same since Jesus died.

Interpretations that engender faith

The entanglement of God
The unsaved Saviour
The communion of the Spirit
The assessment of responsibility (Sin)
The atonement of innocence (Expiation)
The price of people (Redemption)
The washing of hands — or feet? (Cleansing)
The opposition that unites (Reconciliation)
The barriers go down (Access)

13 The Entanglement of God

"God was in Christ, reconciling the world unto himself."
"The Father sent the Son to be the Saviour of the world."
II Corinthians 5:19, I John 4:14

THAT IN JESUS we have seen and known all of the eternal God that finite minds can hope to comprehend, is a familiar and elementary affirmation of Christian faith. In Him God stands revealed, fully, for all time, in ultimate terms. But it is not so often realised how startling is the consequence which Christians have to draw from that basic truth. It was within the shadow of His passion that Jesus said, "He that hath seen me hath seen the Father". And when Paul declares that we have the light of the knowledge of the glory of God in the face of Jesus Christ, believers cannot help remembering that that face was "marred more than the sons of men".

In other words, it is not enough to see God in the Jesus of Bethlehem, Nazareth, and Galilee; we see Him too in the Christ of Golgotha: and the implications are tremendous.

To pagan thought, for example, the idea of a suffering God is simply incredible. Tennyson has enshrined the typical conception in the vow of the Lotos-Eaters to

lie reclined

On the hills like gods together, careless of mankind,
For they lie beside their nectar, and the bolts are hurl'd
Far below them in the valleys, and the clouds are lightly curled
Round their golden houses, girdled with the gleaming world:
Where they smile in secret, looking over wasted lands,
Blight and famine, plague and earthquake, roaring deeps and
*   fiery sands,*
Clanging fights, and flaming towns, and sinking ships, and
*   praying hands.*
But they smile. . . .

That picture of the heartless, indifferent gods imparted to paganism much of its hopelessness and fear; and when better minds

65

strove to rise above the popular conception, it was usually to embrace the still more dreadful creed of a cruel, relentless, impersonal Fate.

Of course there is truth behind the notion that God sits enthroned above the flood, beyond the reach of the storms and conflicts and changes that vex our lives. It is a relief to look away from the decay and uncertainty of life to the God above the struggle, the unshaken Rock beneath which we find shelter, the unassailable Refuge to which we flee, the untroubled Anchorage of our restless hearts.

> *Today and tomorrow with Thee still are Now;*
> *Nor trouble, nor sorrow, nor care, Lord, hast Thou;*
> *Nor passion doth fever, nor age can decay,*
> *The same God for ever that was yesterday.*

There is no imaginable hope or value for our storm-tossed generation in the strange, paradoxical notion of an eternal being struggling to become God, through painful evolution towards divinity.

But, beside that truth of God's transcendence — God the supreme, the "wholly Other" — the Bible sets a second truth: that God stepped down from His unshaken throne above the flood, stepped down amid the storm and pain and mire and sin, to bear our griefs and carry our sorrows — because He cared. The whole difference between ourselves and Him in this respect lies here: that we are in the conflict and the shame largely because we deserve to be, wholly because we cannot help it; He is in it because He *chose* to be. He was immune: He chose, for love's sake to become entangled. We see God upon a cross.

The Old Testament is magnificent in its insistence upon the majestic truth of God's sovereignty, the great King above all gods, Lord of nature, history, and men. It is equally magnificent in its presentation of the more tender truth, that God hears our cry and sees our tears, and knows our sorrows, and "like as a Father", He pitieth His children. "In all their affliction *he was afflicted*" — the suffering God.

Jehovah is the disappointed Husbandman, frustrated by the barren hearts of men. He is the faithful Herdsman, but whereas ox and ass known their master's crib, Israel knoweth not who cares

66

for her. He is the deserted Husband, grieving for His bride. He is the ill-used Father, who in the hour of the son's base ingratitude remembers how He used to hold the little boy's arms and teach him to walk, and in the sharpness of that memory cries out, "O Ephraim, how *can* I let thee go?"

In the New Testament this suffering of the divine sympathy reappears in words and deeds of Jesus. God's vineyard yields no fruit, God's invitation is rudely rejected, the Shepherd grieves for His sheep, the Father watches daily for the prodigal. God has hoped — "Surely, they will reverence my Son" — but man is obdurate. And the deep lament over Capernaum, the tears of Jesus over doomed Jerusalem, tell of the mourning of God for a world unwilling to be saved.

The cross stands thus not only in the midst of human history but in the very heart of God, because God would have it so. How aptly this speaks to our perplexed and saddened generation in this sorrow-laden century!

> *The other gods were strong, but Thou wast weak;*
> *They rode, but Thou didst stumble to a throne:*
> *But to our wounds only gods' wounds can speak,*
> *And not a god has wounds, but Thou alone.*

Reason cries, "If God were good, He could not look upon the sin and misery of man: His heart would break". The Christian points to the cross and says, "His heart did break!" The sceptic declares, "In such a world, how can we keep from sin? It is God's fault; God should be punished!" The Christian kneels and whispers, "God accepted responsibility, and punishment: look at Jesus!" The bitter, defiant rationalism of angry men, full of their own miseries and complaints, can find no answer to this startling light that Calvary throws upon the heart of God. That He is God within the conflict, sharing the pain, standing beside us in our suffering, sitting beside us in our sorrow: this silences unbelief, and heals the smart.

It tells us more, it is true, than just God's sympathy. In the suffering of God for men we measure His deliberate, unswerving purpose to save at all costs. *He* has "given commandment", *He* "spared not His only-begotten", "*the Father* sent the Son to be the Saviour". In the suffering of God through sin we measure also the purity of God. Though the Sin-bearer be His own Son, the sin must be judged, atoned for: inscribed upon the cross we see in flaming letters, God is *just*. For God cannot compromise with evil, anywhere.

In the suffering of God with men we measure too the patience of God. He stoops to plead, Come, let us reason together. He *commends* His love. He yields Himself to the hands of wicked men to win man's faith and love. He cries in human pain, "How can I give thee up?" He was made flesh and dwelt among us, to bear our griefs and carry our sorrows, that we might know His love that will not let us go. Can we hold out against a patience, a persistence, as ardent as this?

An ancient church in central Italy contains a unique portrayal of this profound Christian insight. A more or less conventional painting of the crucifixion emphasises, as did so much early Christian art, the agony of Jesus. But — so it is said — the attentive student will notice strange suggestions of light and shadow about the extremities of the cross, and as he ponders will catch the dim suggestion of a vision of God superimposed upon the crucifix. God too lies, as it were, upon the cross, the Father's hands behind the hands of the Son, the feet of God beneath the feet of Christ, the divine heart coinciding with the Master's heart. And thus the nails which pierced the hands of Jesus passed through the hands of God; and so with feet and spear-thrust: in the passion of the Son, God too was crucified.

If the account be true, the artist has seen deeply the meaning of the gospel. The eternal God, throned in majesty, clothed in glory, is not indifferent to man's suffering and shame: God stepped down, to become involved. "God was in Christ, reconciling the world unto himself." This God is our God, even unto death.

14 The Unsaved Saviour

"He saved others; himself he cannot save."
"Others were tortured, not accepting deliverance."

Matthew 27:42, Hebrews 11:35

EVEN THE INSPIRING eleventh chapter of the epistle to the Hebrews, with all its memories of the great ones in sacred story, contains nothing more magnificent than this comment upon certain who endured torture: they would not accept deliverance. It enshrines the very perfection of courage and loyalty to truth. To run into persecution, loss and peril, and be offered the way out, only to refuse to take it for conscience' sake, is to have passed a supreme test of integrity and strength. We are all prone to sue for peace in any controversy, to search for accommodating formulas which will save our face while evading the principle at issue; the temptation to avoid trouble by at least appearing to agree, or agreeing that perhaps after all the contention does not matter, is present with us all. Then the phrase about the Hebrew martyrs stands up to rebuke us — "not accepting deliverance".

A similar implication lies behind the remark which Matthew preserves of those passed by the crowd at the foot of the cross: "He saved others, himself he cannot save". He too would not accept deliverance, because the price of deliverance was too high. Had He saved Himself, we must have been lost.

The temptation to evade the issue was as real to Jesus as it is to us. He faced it in the wilderness after His baptism, as the tempter offered alternative paths to a throne, by-passing the cross. He faced it at Caesarea Philippi, when Peter protested, "Lord this shall never be unto thee", and Jesus, recognising the Adversary behind the apostle, rebuked him sharply. Beyond the Jordan, when news of Lazarus' illness came to Him, and Thomas urged Him not to return to Judea, the choice of peace or peril had to be made once more; and in Jerusalem when certain Greeks sought audience with Him and the decisive hour is at hand, Jesus cries, "What shall I say? Father save me." Again in the garden of Gethsemane the prayer is costly that ends in "Thy will be

69

done", and already there enters His mind the possibility of deliverance by angels.

Here are six occasions of which we know, when by a resolute act of will He would not save Himself, choosing not to accept deliverance. But of course all the way through He might have kept His silence. He could have stayed at Nazareth, or remained among the crowds in Galilee. He could have continued to avoid the domains of Herod and of Pilate, and omitted contentious acts — like the ride into Jerusalem and the cleansing of the Temple — or contentious words such as the parable of the vineyard. He might, that is to say, have been a very different kind of Jesus: He might have saved Himself — but He would not then have been the Saviour.

There is of course a challenge here to loyalty in costly situations. One thinks of Peter in Jerusalem, offered safety if he will be silent about Jesus, replying, "We cannot but speak. . . " . One thinks of Polycarp, offered his life for a pinch of incense before the image of Caesar, and making answer, "Eighty and six years have I served my King and Saviour, and He has never done me wrong: I cannot deny my King who has saved me". One thinks of Luther, similarly offered an opportunity to recant and similarly not accepting deliverance.

So it has been with the whole long roll of heroes of the unconsenting conscience, who saw that issues sometimes *must* be faced, evils challenged, truth spoken plainly, and who counted faithfulness their first duty. Deliverance is defeat, if the cost be too high; and there are times when evasion may save us a cross at the price of a crown.

But to look a little more deeply, the refusal of Jesus to accept deliverance is a challenge as much to faith as to faithfulness. We so often suppose that if we run into difficulties for conscience' sake, God will get us out of them, unscathed, without loss. We sometimes speak as though that is what God is for! — to vindicate our stand for right, and deliver us from trouble. It seems to us the supreme tragedy of a good life, and a perplexity to faith, when a faithful man such as Jeremiah does not live to see his work bear fruit and his cause upheld.

Yet Jesus went onwards right to death, not praying for divine intervention, nor imagining that His Father had provided this or that way out of danger. His faith did not presuppose deliverance. The greatest faith never does. Probably the bravest words in all the Old Testament are those of Daniel's friends: "Our God, whom we serve, is able to deliver us from the burning fiery furnace, and he will deliver us out of your hand O king. But if not, be it known unto you that we will not serve your gods nor worship the image you have set up".

But if not, if God does *not* deliver: that is faith at its highest stretch. It leaves the issue with God, whether to deliver or not, whether to vindicate or not, and holds straight on its course though the heavens fall. Beneath the cross we learn that deliverance may not come, though God does not desert us, and will be with us to the end. With a world in need and a race to redeem, it may be necessary sometimes for truth to be written in blood and right to be asserted in pain. A word of Ruskin is singularly appropriate here penetrating far into the mind of Jesus and the law of the Christian life in this matter of expecting God's deliverance: "The great mystery of the idea of sacrifice . . . is founded on the secret truth . . . that you cannot save men from death but by facing it for them, nor from sin but by resisting it for them". So! He saved others — that is why He could not save Himself.

More deeply still, there lies in the refusal of Jesus to accept deliverance a challenge to fuller understanding of Himself. For many modern folk the cross is the most perplexing thing about the Master. The Teacher and the teaching we understand, the social Reformer with a vision, the spiritual Mystic uttering divine secrets, the Master with His challenge, the Friend and Comrade of our way. We can, too, find means of fitting into these categories of our thought the story of a tragedy, in which the Teacher is put to death because His truth was yet unwelcome; the Master betrayed, the Friend forsaken. Christ the Hero, the greatest of the world's unjustly treated, and the cross a mistake, a grim and ugly interlude — this we can grasp. But this is not at all His thought about it: He would not accept a way out!

To Jesus, the passion was *necessary*: for this cause He came into the world; the Son of man must suffer; this commandment He received of His Father; His life is laid down for the sheep.

71

To His mind, it was *redemptive*: He came to give His life a ransom for many, and His blood is covenant-blood shed for many for remission. Thus His passion is also, in His thought, *representative*: He bears our sins, pleads for us, dies for us, atones for us, standing in for us and so committing us to stand in at Calvary with Him. For all these reasons, He expects that His death will draw all men unto Him, and usher in the kingdom.

And so the cross destroys our neat and manageable categories of thought, and lifts both Jesus and His death into the realm of uniqueness, of incomparable and lonely majesty as the only Mediator between God and man, the Saviour, the Redeemer, the Lord, the Son of God. Just because He would not save Himself — and *could* not — He out-tops all comparisons. Just because He was born to die, His life defies all parallel.

We stand here, admittedly, on the edge of vast questions about atonement, redemption, and salvation: but even on the edge we can see the direction thought must take. The unbroken sense of a divine constraint that lay upon the heart of Christ, and found repeated expression in phrases like "the Son of man must needs be delivered into the hands of wicked men", "the Son of man *must* suffer", "ought not the Christ to suffer these things?" compels us to accept the cross as the major purpose of His coming. And from that basic thought the path lies clear to fullest, loving, adoring acknowledgement that He is more than Teacher, Mystic, Friend or Hero: He is our Redeeming Lord. He saved *us* — thank God He would not save Himself.

15 The Communion of the Spirit

"I will pray the Father, and he shall give you another Comforter . . . even the Spirit of truth."
"If I go not away, the Comforter will not come unto you. . . . Howbeit when he, the Spirit of truth, is come, he will guide you into all truth."

John 14:16, 17; 16:7, 13

JOHN, IT WOULD APPEAR, is the only one of the evangelists to make the promise of the Spirit a theme for the Lord's Supper. According to his record, Jesus spoke three times of the One whose coming would replace His earthly presence in the experience of the disciples, and expounded with considerable fullness the Spirit's ministry and aim, before He blessed the broken bread and passed the cup of wine among them all. Among all its rich themes for meditation, the Lord's Table reiterates for us this solemn undertaking of the departing Lord, that His Spirit will abide with us "until he come". The Supper is full of the memories of Calvary: but it also points back quite deliberately to Pentecost.

And there are several reasons why this fact must never be obscured. As the Lord's Supper looks back towards a "finished work," so the promise of the Spirit, spoken across the Table, reminds us of His unfinished, continuing ministry. As the Supper speaks with vividness of His death for us, so the promise of the Spirit recalls the continual communication of His life. As the Supper looks forward to His coming, so the promise of the Spirit ensures His presence with us now. As the Supper recalls the gift of peace, the first blessing of the gospel, so the assurance of the Spirit's enduement reminds us we are called to conflict and to toil.

Thus is preserved the proportion of the truth. If we had only the Supper, Christianity might be regarded as at bottom just a pious memory. If we had only the memorial Supper and the promise "till he come", it might be said that Christianity is a memory of Jesus past nourishing a hope of Jesus still to come. But across the Table comes the promise of His indwelling, and Christianity is seen to be a faithful memory nursing a glorious hope while living in the joy of a perpetual fellowship with a present Lord. The gift of the Spirit ensures for the gospel, so to speak, a present tense. And the Lord's Table is first and foremost a Table of Fellowship, not simply with our fellow Christians but with Him. We meet in Christ's name and in His presence, who has come to take up His abode with us.

Moreover, the promise of the Spirit spoken across the Table is also, in an important sense, spoken out of the midst of the Table. That is to say, the promise is framed to meet the need foreshadowed by all that is signified in broken bread and outpoured wine. The disciples probably understood but little of all that Jesus said in the sombre, moving discourse of the upper room; but this at least they grasped quite clearly — Jesus was leaving them, suffering and danger lay ahead, hostility and rejection faced themselves as already it confronted Him.

There was desolation in their hearts at that thought of losing Him: "Because I have spoken these things unto you, sorrow hath filled your hearts". But there was also bewilderment. Nothing was turning out as they expected; much that He said did not make sense to them. It was all too plain that He had many things to say which they could not yet bear.

The prospect facing them, of picking their way anxiously forward, only dimly understanding His great truths, and always beset by their own slowness of apprehension as well as the contradiction of the world, was far from bright. And aside from their own sorrow, and confusion, there were always Pilate, Caiaphas, Rome and Jewry, scoffing relations and sneering acquaintances, to mock all that they had hoped, and lost. As surely as the broken bread and spilled wine foreshadowed Christ's fate, so surely did it foretell their own defeat and danger.

We know that things turned out far otherwise; but that is how the situation appeared to them on the night on which He was betrayed, as with His sad meanings beating on their minds they peered into a grey future without their Lord. And it was to just that situation that He addressed His all-transforming promise: "I will send the Comforter, even the Spirit of truth. . . " . This is His answer to their mood, their fears, their need. Each time the promise is repeated, the double name is purposefully used: Comforter, Spirit of truth: strength is promised, fortitude, to "fortify"

74

their hearts; and insight, understanding, teaching, to illumine their perplexities. And both are given by the endowment of His own Spirit, abiding *in* them always.

The Comforter, or "paraclete", means literally One "called in", or called alongside oneself, to give assistance. In the courts, it means a friend of the accused called in to speak to his character, or otherwise to enlist sympathy on his behalf. And where the "friend" is trained and qualified to do so, the "paraclete" is a barrister, an advocate, pleading for the one in trouble. John uses the word thus of Jesus, our "Advocate with the Father", and the Spirit is described as *"another* Paraclete".

Precisely the same thoughts find expression, with Paul, in the language of the priesthood rather than the courts. Christ is at the right hand of God, making intercession for us; and the Spirit, too, maketh intercession for us, with groanings which cannot be uttered. For the priest, like the barrister, is one called in to plead our cause.

On the battlefield the paraclete is an ally, a relief force, coming in the nick of time to rescue the hard-pressed regiment. In the home, a neighbour or a friend sent for in emergency, is equally a "comforter". Sympathy, or soothing of our feelings, is but a very small part of the ministry of the Spirit: the lovely name implies, rather, practical assistance that makes strong.

In every emergency, whenever the disciples had been accused, beset, despondent, Jesus had been there to counsel, to explain, to speak in their defence, to strengthen faith. Now as He departs, He promises Another, who will give the same support, the gentle sympathy, the glowing thought and strong encouragement, the wise reply, and bold resistance, that they had found in Him. He was not leaving them leaderless, "orphans", unrepresented, friendless: another Comforter would reinforce their wavering will, nerve their timid spirit, uphold their slipping feet, assist their prayers. Across His Table our Lord promises His Spirit to maintain their *strength*: we would not be so burdened, so despondent, so oft-defeated, if we remembered that.

And the source of strength is truth. Doubt and confusion weaken, and the uncertain heart is prey to many fears: so Jesus promises the Spirit of truth, who shall guide them into all truth. With astonishing completeness, the promise of intellectual enlightenment is unfolded to them. "He will bring all things to your remembrance" — to that we owe the Gospels. "He will take of the things of mine and show them unto you" — to that we owe the Epistles. "He will lead you into all truth", which is more than saying, "He will tell you everything": for the deepest truth cannot be learned by being told, but only as God and life educate the soul willing to be led. "And he shall show you things to come." What more could confused and questioning minds require? Memory, interpretation, insight, prophecy: their intellectual equipment was to be complete!

Meanwhile, towards the outside world, He should be the power behind their testimony. As He spoke comfortably to the disciples, so should He speak convictingly to the world, convincing of the sinfulness of sin, the rightness of righteousness, the certainty of judgement. The Spirit will illumine them, and others through them; remove their own confusion and confound their enemies; serve the truth alike in those who love it and in those who will not hear — bring to the one, comfort, to the other, condemnation.

It is hard to see how the promise of the Spirit, spoken across the Table to the situation the Table represented, could possibly be more relevant or complete. Here all is offered that can be needed, and guaranteed by Jesus' prayer and Jesus' blood. Why then do we find the promise only partially fulfilled? Is it because we have not *expected* enough? Or are the conditions unfulfilled? The Spirit cannot come to those who do not know the Christ, nor comfort those who do not love Him, nor enlighten those who do not keep His words. "The world cannot receive because it seeth him not, neither knoweth him. . . . If ye love me, keep my commandments, and I will pray the Father . . . . If a man love me he will keep my words . . . and we will make our abode with him." It is as simple as that!

16 The Assessment of Responsibility

"Ye men of Israel, hear these words; Jesus of Nazareth, a man approved of God among you . . . ye have taken, and by wicked hands have crucified and slain."
"Father, forgive them, for they know not what they do."
Acts 2:22, 23, Luke 23:34

HERE, AT FIRST SIGHT, appear to be two contrary judgements concerning human responsibility for the death of Jesus. Peter pronounces the verdict which generations of Christians unhesitatingly endorsed: Jesus died by the hands of wicked men, Judas, Caiaphas, Pilate, "the Jews".

Judas' part was small. Christ's death was decided upon before the traitor offered his assistance; he merely revealed where Jesus could be arrested without the intervention of the crowd. The acceptance of coin made his comparatively unimportant treachery even more squalid. The prepared plot, and his continued presence among the disciples awaiting opportunity, emphasise his deliberate purpose; behind these, months of frustrated ambition and hardening disagreement prepared for the eventual decision to save his own skin by going over to the enemy. For that, Judas carries tragic responsibility.

Caiaphas sought to defend the tradition, the institutions, the political security of his people, and incidentally his own High Priestly privileges, by getting rid of Jesus. Whether Messiah had come, or God was doing some new thing, Caiaphas did not enquire. That his expediency was wholly selfish, cynical and unjust; that it involved bribery and blackmail, false evidence and deceitful alteration of the charge; that in fearing Rome he forgot to fear God, he did not consider. It is never expedient to do wrong: for his policy and its outcome Caiaphas bears heavy blame.

The supreme responsibility is Pilate's. His was the ultimate decision; he was present in Palestine to administer justice. He understood Christ's claim to kingship in the realm of truth, he believed Christ innocent. Moreover, he wanted to release Him, trying five times to compromise or evade decision. But the demand of the crowd and the threat of Caiaphas forced him to choose between his own security and Christ's. Trapped by his fear of adverse report to Caesar, his previous record of violent misrule, his sense of justice and his superstition, Pilate's courage breaks, and with fury in his heart he delivers Jesus to be crucified. For selfish cowardice and injustice Pilate must ever bear the major part of blame.

With these three must stand indicted the Jerusalem crowd. Five days earlier many had shouted, "Hosanna to the Son of David"; now they support the charge of treason — and demand release of a traitor! Unreasoning acceptance of the Sanhedrin's overnight action, and resentment against re-examination of their verdict, rally the crowd to Caiaphas' side; hysteria, coupled with the mob's usual repudiation of responsibility, does the rest. But for their attitude, Caiaphas could not have forced Pilate's hand, and they share heavy responsibility for Jesus' suffering.

The soldiers' mockery, the bystanders' jeers, witnesses' lies, Peter's denial, all added something to His pain; each in his measure shares in the guilt of Calvary.

This certainly is the view of New Testament thinkers. Christians have no reason to be proud of the spirit of vengeance which for centuries made the Jew despised and proscribed throughout Christendom: but the underlying judgement that men of that race and generation were morally responsible for the cross was true to scripture and to fact. He was indeed taken with wicked hands and *cruelly* put to death by sinful men.

But does not Jesus' word express a wholly different attitude? Does He not say, "They know not what they do"? And is not this in close accord with modern feelings about wrongdoing?

It is certainly the modern fashion to condone evil and undermine responsibility. We blame the social pressures of the age for each individual act of wrong: we blame history, and inherited problems and tensions. We explore psychology to explain away moral freedom in terms of psycho-physical "mechanism", leaving the soul "helpless" in the control of genes and gastric juices.

We rewrite the verdicts of past ages, attempting to prove that moral values are illusions: Judas is but the perfect example of economic man; Caiaphas personifies social control; not Pilate, but Pilate's forebears crucified Jesus. Never has any age so industriously and ingeniously set about proving its own irresponsibility.

We should, of course, be grateful for enlightened treatment of offenders, and a more intelligent sympathy with the fallen, but the repudiation of blame has gone too far. Understanding cannot replace judgement: evil is still evil. The moral sense reasserts itself in spite of all our self-deception.

Paul Tillich has shrewdly remarked that the deep sources of human sinfulness were also known to apostolic writers. When all sympathetic explanations are exhausted the moral re-education of the evil-doer is still imposed by Society, an imposition only justified on grounds of moral responsibility. If none are responsible for what they do, none can be punished, praised or reformed; and the human predicament is desperate indeed.

It was asserted a generation ago that "modern man is too busy to worry about his sins". It was easy to retort that in that case modern man *is* too busy. Reinhold Niebuhr, who more than any other has plumbed the depths of our twentieth-century malaise, has said that one of the most tragic symptoms of the breakdown of the West is "the complacent conscience of modern men in an age of social decay". Denial of responsibility in face of doom may be the ultimate irresponsibility that *deserves* destruction.

It is at least arguable that modern man is beginning to worry quite considerably about his sins. The twentieth century has taught us by dread experience, by costly failure, and by the science of the mind, that what is wrong with the world is man himself. We have learned serious things about evil's vicious circle, about sin's slow destruction of society and the individual, about the intellectual cancer of materialistic atheism that rots the moral fibre of society and the soul.

We call two witnesses to this new sense of moral responsibility. In a review of modern fiction J. Isaacs finds symbols of our time in the catchwords "human predicament", "frustration", "maladjustment", "decadence", "anxiety", "guilt", and "sin". He sees everywhere symptoms of "the weight of modern anxiety, compounded of a strange medley of guilt" and suggests it began with the guilt of the industrial revolution. It peers through the work of Galsworthy, was present earlier in Samuel Butler, mounts through war and wilful blindness, through Belsen, Buchenwald, gas chambers, mass graves and the atom bomb. "In our age", as reflected in fiction, "almost everybody is neurotic, and the whole civilised world is having a nervous breakdown."

Writing just after the Munich agreement with Hitler, T. S. Eliot said, "I believe there must be many . . . to whom that month brought a profounder realisation of our general plight. The feeling which was new and unexpected [was] a feeling of humiliation which seemed to demand an act of personal contrition, of humility, repentance and amendment. What had happened was something in which one was deeply implicated and *responsible*" (*Idea of a Christian Society*).

Apart altogether from political opinions implied, this is not the language of easygoing excusal of evil things — or of pretended human helplessness. Amid the pressures and peril of our present age men are returning to the New Testament insight about personal guilt and the reality of sin; beginning to see that human responsibility for human wrongdoing is an intractable and sobering fact.

Here beneath the cross, we stand in the deep shadow of its darkest truth. Man is *responsible* before history and before God, for what man does. Calvary *exposes* human sin — as no other event in the experience of the race exposes it. Judas sinned against the light of a great opportunity and a glorious friendship; Caiaphas, against all the long revelation symbolized in his sacred office. Pilate sinned against all his training in just administration, and his knowledge of Christ's innocence; the crowd, against the grace of three years' selfless ministry.

And Jesus died, victim of man's sin against light and love and innocence; sacrificed to cowardice, selfishness, ingratitude; broken by corporate wrongdoing in which all share blame, yet each claims personal innocence; killed by the "little" sins that accumulate to a whole world's undoing.

It is indeed a solemn parable: "Father *forgive them*, for they know not what they do". That is what needs forgiveness. He has been so long time with them, and yet have they not known Him, nor have we. This is the final measure of responsibility — rejection of His truth; this is their condemnation and our own — preference for darkness rather than His light.

Sin in the cross is exposed, cauterized, and cleansed. It does its worst, and is defeated: it unveils its dire malignancy, but cannot overcome the love of Christ. Yet all the interweaving melodies of redemption, forgiveness, security and peace, the joyous descant of the hope of glory, sound against the deep bass undertone: He was despised, and rejected of men. This is the measure of sin's power, and the world's perilous predicament. We dare not — for our safety — ever forget man's inhumanity to the Son of Man.

17 The Atonement of Innocence

"Dost thou not fear God, seeing thou art in the same condemnation? And we indeed justly; for we receive the due reward of our deeds: but this man hath done nothing amiss."

Luke 23:40, 41

ONLY RARELY, one supposes, does the conversation of thieves contribute to theology. Yet as we eavesdrop beneath the cross we hear one express to another the central, penetrating truth about the passion of our Lord: "We suffer indeed justly, but this man hath done nothing amiss".

Here is proved crime meeting its due punishment, and innocence alongside it meeting precisely the same end.

What knowledge lay behind the words we cannot tell. Pilate had declared, "I find no fault in this man". Those who had lived with Jesus affirmed, "He did no sin — knew no sin — was without sin — in Him was no sin", and in that conviction worshipped Him as God. Behind their faith stood the verdict of the Most High: "This is my Beloved, in whom I am well pleased".

Thus He is acquitted — and condemned. In Him God is well pleased, yet it pleased the Lord to bruise Him. What justice is this — what does it mean?

The ancient answer is not far to seek. Legend and myth alike demanded the innocent maiden, the unspoiled youth, to stand in peril for the city. The instinct requiring it is old as humanity, deep as the sense of sin. "Wherewith shall I come before the Lord . . . . with thousands of rams? . . . shall I give my firstborn for my transgression, the fruit of my body for the sin of my soul?" enquires the prophet, voicing the belief of a thousand years that the sacrifice of the innocent redeems the guilty.

Here paganism assuaged its panic fears, and expressed a primitive sense of retribution in the savage ordeal by pain. Here the age-old institution of sacrifice, human and animal, found its strength. Nowhere had that institution greater power or truth than in ancient Judaism — the morning and evening sacrifices, the sin-offering, the scapegoat, the day of atonement, guarding the

82

solemn principle that life alone can redeem life, and "without the shedding of blood there is no remission".

Is it surprising that the first Christians so interpreted the passion of our Lord? When Jesus died, sacrifice ended for those who understood: a felt religious need had been fulfilled. They had learned that sin demands atonement, wrong done must be paid for, guilt is only annulled in judgement — somewhere. A loving heart forgives, but out of pain. How natural then to construe the cross in terms of sacrifice and say, "The chastisement of our peace was laid on him. . . . He bore the sin of many. He is the propitiation . . . for the sins of the whole world. He put away sin by the sacrifice of himself, being made sin for us". This is why guilty and innocent hang side by side.

This is assuredly the ancient explanation:

> *Not all the blood of beasts*
> *On Jewish altars slain*
> *Could give the guilty conscience peace*
> *Or wash away the stain.*

> *But Christ, the heavenly Lamb,*
> *Takes all our guilt away*
> *A sacrifice of nobler name*
> *And richer blood than they.*

But we have been told for a long time now that modern minds have difficulty with these ideas — of sacrifice, atonement and expiation for sin. Certainly we should have difficulty with some of the ways in which the truth has been expressed. An angry God, demanding to be pacified with offerings, is not a Christian conception, either of God the Father, or of Calvary. It was because God loved, He gave His Son; it is God who "commendeth his love toward us in that while we were yet sinners, Christ died for us". The notion of a cross-grained Deity needing to be placated is utterly wrong.

But is atonement, expiation, sacrifice, therefore a false idea? To that two answers must be given.

The first is, that the travail and torment and tragedy of the twentieth century have led more thoughtful minds back to the old language of expiation and of judgement.

I call three witnesses. The first is Albert Schweitzer, speaking of the injuries inflicted by the white man on the black: "We and our civilisation are burdened, really, with a great debt. We are not free to confer benefits on these men or not, as we please; it is our duty. Anything we give them is not benevolence but atonement. . . . When we have done all that is in our power, we shall not have atoned for the thousandth part of our guilt".

The second witness is Eleanor Rathbone. Writing to friends in India when the battle of Britain had been fought and the ordeal by bombing had been endured, she said, "Now we are no longer ashamed. We feel that if there is anything in the doctrine of expiation, Britain has expiated her sin".

And the third is Jerrard Tickell's harrowing story of Odette "Churchill" — British agent in occupied France. Captured, tortured and imprisoned, she was offered some easing of her suffering, but refused. She believed that "by electing to stay in her cell, and by continuing without bitterness to withstand loneliness, cold, hunger and pain, she was helping in a most humble way to take from mankind a tiny particle of the vast necessary burden of human suffering. She had come to believe there was a fixed and bitter price to be paid by humanity for humanity, and to her had been given the glory of contributing in minute measure to that sum".

One recalls with these the confession of T. S. Eliot concerning the dark days of 1938, of a sense of something "which seemed to demand contrition, humility, repentance, amendment". Here are *modern* minds, led back by hard experience and by suffering, to ancient insights about evil — and its cost. Here is the age-old language re-minted in our time — a price to be paid, amendment, contrition, repentance, expiation. These are gospel categories of thought: the terminology of atonement. We have been made to think again: to discover forgiveness is not easy, and sin extracts its penalty, somewhere, sometime. We have learned to measure the *cost* of the world's redemption — and the price is expiation.

The other thing to be said goes deeper still. We have learned not only the cost but the *difficulty* of saving a world from sin. We thought once that enlightenment would do it: science, education, psychology between them would redeem the world. Some of us even thought that preaching would do it. Now we know better.

84

We have found that it is not ideas — self-interest, fear, the social good — that save a man: but *deeds*.

Ideas inspire, but deeds redeem. Loving deeds, costly deeds, identifying the innocent with the guilty in redemptive service — these are the forces of salvation. Vincent de Paul takes his place beside the prisoners chained for life to the rowlocks, that he might win their trust. Damien lives and dies among the lepers, to gain their souls. Freemen sell themselves into slavery, to capture the slave's love and break the tyranny.

In the Middle Ages the Flagellants — bands of religious zealots fifty to a hundred strong — marched through Europe: nine thousand passed through Strasburg in three months. At every stopping place, with whips barbed with iron, they publicly flogged each other in penitence for sin. Out of that strange exaggeration of a valid principle, came the nobler impulse. Monks did penance for others' sin, nuns accepted prison sentences for wayward girls, godly men and women pleaded to be allowed to take condemnation for wrong their neighbours did.

Certainly it worked. Those who could withstand all else could not resist a love like this. In a French reformatory one wild lad stabbed another, and was condemned by the boys themselves, to three months in a darkened cell. The guilty boy was terrified. The wounded boy then volunteered to serve the sentence for him, and the masters agreed, provided that the guilty one should take him bread and water. He did it for six days — and then broke down, begging to take the punishment himself, a changed, subdued and penitent soul.

All over the world the principle holds: in every land are those who in obedience to the spirit of the cross have plunged into the Tokio slums, into Africa's shanty-towns, into the forest and darkness, into the vice and violence of the West, each accepting conditions he does not deserve, to win the love of those who do deserve — by all means to save some; not holding aloof in innocence, but identified with evil things, and filling up what remains of the redemptive suffering of Christ.

Only so can stubborn, wilful hearts be changed. And it is the way God chose. He bore our sins in His own body on the tree. The Lord hath laid on Him the iniquity of us all. Of course He had done nothing amiss, but we had!

He dies to atone for sins not His own
Your debt He has paid and your work He has done:

Ye all may receive the peace He did leave —
Who made intercession, My Father forgive.

"The just for the unjust" — there is no other basis for atonement. Nor is there any easier way to win the world for Christ.

18   The Price of People

"Then one of the twelve, called Judas Iscariot, went unto the chief priests, and said unto them, What will ye give me, and I will deliver him unto you? And they covenanted with him for thirty pieces of silver."
"Ye were not redeemed with corruptible things, as silver and gold . . . but with the precious blood of Christ."
Matthew 26:14, 15, I Peter 1:18, 19

IT IS DOUBTLESS only an accident that the shape of the Christian cross roughly resembles the outline of a pair of beam scales, the upright stanchion supporting a balanced cross-beam. But accident or no, the similarity enshrines a truth: for there as nowhere else in history, souls were weighed in the balance, and their worth compared.

The slave-market where buyers haggle over the purchase of their fellow men has always seemed an offence to dignity and humanity. There is something inherently wrong about setting a price to people. So it is that few things in the story of Christ's passion have caught the imagination more than the miserable bargain Judas made with the chief priests. Whatever excuse we might otherwise have found for it, the thirty pieces of silver reduce his betrayal to the sordid and selfish selling of a friend. So Matthew deliberately sets the deed of Judas alongside the generous gift of Mary in anointing Jesus' feet with precious spikenard, and alongside Judas' own professed concern for the needs of the *poor!*

It was of course the customary price of a slave. Joseph was sold by his brethren for twenty pieces, but the Midianites had still to make a profit! So these priests and this disciple weighed the worth of Jesus at the value of a slave, revealing only the poverty of their own standards.

Do not blame Judas only. Caiaphas weighed Jesus against the worth of his own position and pride, and counted Him less. Pilate weighed Jesus against the might and glory of Caesar, and threw Jesus away. The crowd weighed Jesus against the violent, blood-stained adventurer Barabbas, and chose Barabbas. All agreed with

Judas in the value they set upon the Son of God. He was the stone which the builders rejected, not perceiving His worth; He was despised and rejected of men, who saw no beauty in Him that they should desire Him. They weighed Him in their little selfish, materialist, worldly balances, and found Him wanting: they knew no better.

A seventeenth century poet, Joseph Beaumont, makes the fitting comment:

> But thou, improvident Judas, since thou art
> Resolved to sell a thing whose value is
> Beyond the power of arithmetic art
> To reckon up — proportionate thy price
>   In some more near degree; let thy demand
>   Make buyers, who this Christ is, understand.
>
> Ask all the gold that rolls on Indus' shore,
> Ask all the treasures of the Eastern Sea,
> Ask all the earth's yet undiscovered ore,
> Ask all the gems and pearls which purest be,
>   Ask Herod's 'chequer, ask the high priest's crown,
>   Ask Caesar's mighty sceptre and his throne.
>
> Ask all the silver of the glistering stars,
> Ask all the gold that flames in Phoebus' eyes,
> Ask all the jewels of Aurora's tears,
> Ask all the smiles and beauties of the skies,
>   Ask all that can by any thing be given,
>   Ask bliss, ask life, ask paradise, ask heaven.
>
> Urge him no more with sense and reason; he
> Resolves to traffic with the priests; for now
> No other god but money he can see —
> He nothing sees at all, and cares not how
>   He makes his bargain with them, so he may
>   Have but this wretched sum in ready pay.

A bad bargain, beside which Esau's trading of his birthright for a mess of pottage was just a silly miscalculation!

Yet Jesus so often warns us against precisely that miscalculation of the true worth of things. The farmer, satisfied with life's success because his barns were full and his bank account in balance, is a "fool", because he is not rich toward God. Dives ignores Lazarus at his gate, yet eagerly would exchange places with him in the after-life. The pearls and treasures of experience are to be found in life under God's rule, but men prefer the husks which the swine do eat. We are anxious about what to eat and what to put on, and fail to set our hearts on the kingdom of God as the *supreme* value.

And so moth and rust corrupt, and thieves break through and steal, the hoarded wealth of human hearts ignorant that the only safe treasure is in heavenly things. How often Jesus said these things: how often they needed to be said, when men could conspire to sell God's loveliest Gift for thirty pieces of silver.

But there is a happier aspect of this pricing of souls at Calvary. Besides their valuation of Him is set His valuation of us. They held Him cheap: He counted us precious. Judas sold Him for thirty shekels; He purchased us, not with corruptible things such as silver and gold, but with His precious blood. Caiaphas, Herod, Pilate, the crowds dismissed Him as worthless; looking upon us with a Redeemer's eyes He held there is not a soul on earth but is worth a Christ's ransom. He set on their heads, and on ours, the price of His own pain: He weighed their souls, and ours, and found He wanted them.

This too He had so often said: ye are of more *value* than many sparrows, although not a sparrow falls to the ground without your Father knowing. Man's needs — hunger, health — took precedence over the holy Sabbath and the sacred law, for they are designed for man. Man's soul is worth more than all the world, and to gain the world's prizes by its loss is to achieve no profit. There is nothing a man can give in equal exchange for his soul; he is the most precious thing in reach.

And when the soul is imperilled through sin then in His eyes "the redemption of their soul is precious". The shepherd will seek the sheep until he find it, for its value's sake. The woman will search the coin, because it is worth finding. The father watches for the son because he is dear to him. The gospel attitude to sinners is never sentimental, but a Christlike valuation of people. As God could say of Israel, "I gave Egypt for thy ransom. Since thou wast precious in my sight. . ." , so Jesus could say of all the world, "The Son of man came, not to be ministered unto, but to minister, and to give his life a ransom for many".

He redeemed us at a price; that is the measure of His claim upon us. The apostles draw out the implications of that valuation in several forthright ways. We are not our own, but bought with a price, and must glorify God in our body and in our spirit, which are God's. To take back our members, possessions, talents, lives, from the service of Him who redeemed us, is to "deny the Lord who bought us".

Because we are His we are responsible to Him alone. That is our freedom: to our own Master we stand and fall. We are His servants, and must not be bondslaves to any man, neither cringing before criticism, nor sensitive to scorn, nor enslaved by opinions. We are to do all things as serving the Lord. We are His slaves, sealed with His Spirit, though not the spirit of bondage; branded with His sign, bearing in ourselves the marks of the Lord Jesus, in the scars of many a battle for Him.

"He gave his life a ransom": that is also the measure of His care for us. He has made us precious for all time, because He counted us — only God knows why — worth the saving. And He cares for His own. We are sealed unto the day of redemption, and He will surely claim what He has purchased at such cost. In the Apocalypse, the sealing of the Lord's own is a means of protection to those whose safety the Lord will require at the hand of the enemy. Therein lies our sure security, the pledge of final salvation. We are His and He will not let us go.

Thirty shekels of silver, and the precious blood of Christ! How differently men value things. He who is priceless they sold for a song; and we who are worthless He freely redeemed by a King-of-king's ransom. We are aghast at the value they dared to set upon Him: we are silenced and humbled at the infinite value He chose to set upon us. In the scales of the cross all values are changed: we only know that by the price He paid we are gladly His, now and for ever.

19   The Washing of Hands — or Feet?

"Pilate . . . took water, and washed his hands before the multi-tude, saying, I am innocent of the blood of this just person: see ye to it."
"Jesus poureth water into a bason and began to wash the disciples' feet."

Matthew 27:24, John 13:5

FROM THE TIME of Pilate to the present day, "washing one's hands" has been accepted as the appropriate gesture for repudiating responsibility when things get difficult.   Pilate was cornered, between Caesar, Caiaphas, Christ and the crowd: to evade the dilemma he declares it is not his business; he cannot help what is happening.   He "washes his hands" of the whole affair.

It is an attitude of mind the twentieth century understands. With a few noble exceptions, scientists disown responsibility for the consequences of the work "society" asks them to do.   Govern-ments deny responsibility for the drift of world affairs; journalists and entertainers refuse to be blamed for supplying what the low standard of public taste makes profitable.   "Angry young men" refuse responsibility for "inherited" problems.   Certain distorted exaggerations of psychology have "excused" bad behaviour on the ground of moral helplessness.   Never was the demand for deter-gents so insistent.   We, as a generation, are experts in "getting out from under" our deserts.   From the Great Powers, deadlocked in mutual recrimination and abuse, to the pathetic weakling be-fore the Court pleading, "I could not help it: I was drunk", the futile gesture of self-cleansing by washing one's hands of respon-sibility runs through our society.

Of course it *is* futile.   In *The Man Born to be King* Miss Dor-othy Sayers powerfully reminded us that in every generation, in every language, through every century since the first, men have chanted, whispered, sung or proclaimed that Jesus "suffered under Pontius Pilate".   He might wash his hands a hundred times: they carry still the stain of Jesus' blood.

Inevitably arises the memory of Lady Macbeth:

> *Look, how she rubs her hands.*
> *It is an accustomed action with her, to seem thus washing her hands.*
> *Out, damned spot! out I say.* . . . *What, will these hands ne'er be clean?*
> *Here's the smell of the blood still: all the perfumes of Arabia will not sweeten this little hand.*

And Macbeth, himself a later Pilate:

> *How is't with me, when every noise appals me?*
> *What hands are here?* . . .
> *Will all great Neptune's ocean wash this blood*
> *Clean from my hand? No, this my hand will rather*
> *The multitudinous seas incarnadine*
> *Making the green one red.*

No man can *ever* cleanse himself. We gesture in vain; responsibility remains till God absolves.

And He does. Beside the picture of Pilate vainly washing his hands of all responsibility for Jesus, is set another portrait — of Jesus, vicariously washing the feet of His disciples, accepting responsibility — all their responsibilities — as His own, *making them clean*. He will not wash His hands of them, even of Peter, or Thomas, or Judas: instead, He washed their feet. And when one demurred, He spoke in tones of firmness and authority, words that illumine one aspect of the cross: "Except I wash thee, thou hast no part with me".

Jewish ritual made much of cleansing, in the priestly preparation for sacrifice, and the people's care for cleanness of body and of clothes in approaching the sanctuary. A holy God demands a pure people. The bathing of proselytes entering Judaism from pagan faiths, the baptism of repentance which John preached, the "washing of regeneration" by "water and the Word" of the apostolic church — all enshrine the same conception. "Your hands are full of blood," declared Isaiah; "wash you, make you clean . . . cease to do evil, learn to do well. . . ." "Wash me thoroughly from mine iniquity and cleanse me from my sin" is David's prayer. "I will sprinkle clean water upon you," Ezekiel promises, and Zechariah foresees a fountain opened for all uncleanness.

"Who shall ascend the hill of the Lord? . . . He that hath clean hands." "The pure in heart" — in thought, imagination, desire, — "see God". This is an axiom of Biblical religion. The world is soiled and stained, and the hands and hearts of men unclean and God is holy. A Gospel of cleansing is the only answer: "Except I wash thee, thou hast no part with me".

Nor is this language merely ancient, outworn metaphor. In this as in so many things, new knowledge is catching up with old insights. We understand more exactly than our fathers the nature of defilement but they knew well how necessary was spiritual purification. The older language spoke of cleansing before God. The sense of guilt, tinged with fear, evoked *remorse,* which against a background of vivid belief in hell, cried out for pardon, for mercy, for a "theological" cleansing, so to speak, in relationship with God. The newer emphasis is upon cleansing from wrongdoing itself, a "psychological" purification of memory and imagination, a removal of the subconscious defilement which practised sin produces, the repressed moral inferiority complex that makes one disgusted with oneself, festers in the soul, paralyses the will, confuses the conscience, and makes the whole life cynical and bitter. What is all this, but psychiatry's version of the ancient religious wisdom, such as David knew: "Behold, thou desirest truth in the inward parts: purge me . . . and I shall be clean, wash me and I shall be whiter than snow: create in me a clean heart, O God, and renew a right spirit within me. . . ". And Saul of Tarsus: "I know that in me (that is, in my flesh) dwelleth no good thing: sin dwelleth in me".

Transgression punishes the sinner, not only hereafter but here, in himself. Evil *defiles* the evildoer; wrong *stains* the soul that practises it, sin *soils* the sinning life. And the urgent need is not just to "drag the hidden thing into the daylight of consciousness", which is psychiatry's version of Christian penitence and confession: but to add to this a real cleansing, a deep renewal, a deep-reaching purification that shall recreate the soul.

This Christ undertakes to do. He says to all, as He said to lepers, "I will . . . be thou clean!" The testimony of those who let Him save, is clear: "If any man be in Christ, he is a new creature"; "if we confess our sins he is faithful and just to forgive us our sins *and to cleanse us*".

> There is a fountain, filled with blood
> Drawn from Immanuel's veins;
> And sinners, plunged beneath that flood,
> Lose all their guilty stains.

We must be careful not to let the truth evaporate in the familiarity of the terms. In the Upper Room, around the Table, Jesus left no doubt of the thoroughness of the cleansing. The cup recalls the covenant-blood He shed for many for *remission* of sins — that is cleansing before God. He speaks too of the disciples as "clean through the word which I have spoken unto you" — that is cleansing of the mind, by truth. Again, with change of figure, but not of meaning, He discourses on the "purging" of the vine that it might be more fruitful — that is the cleansing through discipline, till the outer life be spotless. He promises the Spirit — of holiness and truth — to dwell with purifying power within the soul itself. And He distinguishes the general cleansing — "bathing" — of those who accept remission, from the *continual* washing of the feet repeatedly defiled along the way — the daily forgiveness of the penitent heart that knows itself sincere but not yet sinless.

Such is the total cleansing He makes the condition of "having part" with Him. Admittedly, that is no easy demand for modern men. Penitence is not a fashionable virtue. Infinitely easier is it, to sit like Mary before our Lord, and wash His feet in service, anoint them with our love. The time will come for that, too. But it is not for that He asks: but, first, that we let Him wash us, from guilt, defilement and all uncleanness; then that we wash the feet of one another.

The former is difficult because it demands acknowledgement that we need cleansing, and cannot cleanse ourselves. The latter is hard, because it implies so much of lowly service, friendship without reserve, giving way to one another, and helping to cleanse the stained and unlovely. Certainly we shall never do the second till we have let Him do the first, and purge us of our pride.

But we have little choice, when all is said. Either we stand with vain and foolish Pilate wringing our hands in pitiable, futile protest that "it was not our fault — we could not help it!" Or we sit with Peter, in repentant humility and adoring faith, and say, "Lord, not my feet only, but also my hands, and my head".

For Jesus said: "Except I wash thee, thou hast no part with me".

20 *The Opposition that Unites*

"And the same day Pilate and Herod were made friends together:
for before they were at enmity between themselves."
"God was in Christ, reconciling the world unto himself."

Luke 23:12, II Corinthians 5:19

SOME STRANGE ALLIANCES were formed around the cross of Jesus.
Herod's family had once ruled Palestine for the Romans and resented the appointment of procurators in Judea.   Pilate had once
at least invaded Galilee to suppress revolt, treading upon Herod's
toes, and suspected that Herod sent secret reports to Caesar about
Jewish affairs. Yet against Jesus they are united, and that fateful
day become "friends".

"The Pharisees went forth, and straightway took counsel with
the Herodians against Jesus, how they might destroy him."   Again
irreconcilables join hands! For while Herodians supported Rome,
and everything Greek or Roman, excusing Herod's infamous im-
moralities, the Pharisees opposed all foreign influence and maintained a most rigorous puritanism.   Yet these too find common
cause in putting Christ to death.

Add to these Caiaphas, declaring publicly to a Roman governor,
amid Passover memories of ancient liberation, "We have no king
but Caesar!"   Caiaphas and Caesar, Israel and Rome — strange
friendship indeed!

"They that passed by reviled him. . . . Likewise also the chief
priests mocking him, with the scribes and elders . . . the thieves
also, which were crucified with him, cast the same in his teeth."
Priests, scribes, elders, "the thieves also": a curious unity, but at
one in their judgement of Jesus.

Saddest example of all, a disciple joins hands with the Sanhedrin
in a sordid, selfish, sneaking compact made in secret between men
with nothing else in common but antagonism to Christ.

"The Jews require a sign, and the Greeks seek after wisdom" —
a difference fundamental and far-reaching — yet is the cross to the
Jews a stumblingblock, to the Greeks foolishness.   In all else poles
apart, in this they are agreed, that the cross of Jesus is to be
despised.

These are all unnatural alliances against the Christ. The cross seems to bind even its enemies together; these are not the last unsanctified friendships in which Christ has been crucified. At one time a shallow-minded Church, anxious for popularity, tried to baptise into Christ mythologies and idolatries that corrupted the gospel and hid the Christ. At another, Christian leaders, weary of persecution and jealous of power, gained political establishment at the price of spiritual purity.

Personal friendships can be a great help in Christian life, or sometimes a great hindrance. When friendship, perhaps deepening into courtship, ripening into marriage, can only proceed upon the assumption that Christ is tacitly forgotten, then once again Pilate and Herod are doing their deal, Judas is making his covenant, and Caiaphas and Caesar are joining hands against the Lord.

But this, of course, is not the whole of the matter. Listen again! "Now there stood by the cross of Jesus his mother, and Mary Magdalene" — friends at the cross. So John, the beloved disciple, who leaned on Christ's breast at the holy supper, the apostle of love joins a Roman centurion, a man trained to arms in the sternest school in history, devoted to Caesar, to testify in words of wonder: "Truly this man was a son of God".

Later Paul was to write to the Ephesians of the continuing miracle of reconciliation enacted before their eyes, as Jew and Gentile joined hands in prayer, sang together of their faith in Christ, and passed the bread and wine from hand to hand in memory of the night on which He was betrayed by Jews and crucified by Gentiles. The spectacle of master and slave, a citizen of the Empire sitting next to one without rights, property, dignity or family was no less startling, even disturbing, to the pagan world.

A Japanese officer, bursting in upon a reported secret meeting of Chinese "resistance leaders" found them gathered around an open book, a cup of wine and a broken loaf. They started up in fear: he stopped in sudden shame and embarrassment; then swiftly stripping off his uniform jacket, he knelt with them to pray, and accepted from their hands the symbols of a friendship deeper than the strife of nations could break. The significant thing is that such a story might be true.

This, certainly, is true. Through long years of childhood a young missionary had dreamed of the mission field, prayed and studied, trained and pleaded and travelled at last across the seas, eager and earnest and dedicated beyond a doubt. But never, she said, never once did the whole amazing, romantic, compelling truth of the missionary achievement dawn upon her soul until she sat at last in the Baptist Church in Calcutta, just after the second war, between a Chinese pastor and a Japanese teacher, a few Americans in front of her, and a German doctor behind, English colleagues on the dais, a Swedish missionary conducting the service amid a congregation of Indian Christians — and all eating the same bread, drinking the same cup, thinking the same thoughts, loving the same Lord. There, she saw and felt and knew the power of Calvary to bridge the gulfs that separate men from each other and from God.

Mary of Nazareth and Mary Magdalene — what a gulf of morality! John the beloved and the Roman centurion — what a gulf of outlook! Jew and pagan, how deep the divisions of race and religion! Master and slave, Chinese and Japanese, East and West — all the bedevilling divisions that afflict mankind dissolve when men confront the cross of Christ, and find what Piers Plowman found so long ago

> Blood brothers did we all become there,
> And gentlemen each one.

For the cross of Jesus has bound together not only His plotting enemies but His remembering friends, in a fellowship more deep and enduring than anything on earth.

Yet this again is not the ultimate truth of the matter. In ways beyond our clear defining the same cross brings together not merely man and his fellow but man and his God. This is the biggest miracle of all, but of its reality every pardoned, purified, reconciled heart can testify.

Miracle? — yes, because the cross of Jesus speaks first and loudly of hostility, the alienation of men from God. Plainly the cross declares the vehement resolution of human hearts: "We will not have this man reign over us". In the awful words of Jesus, they had both seen and hated both Him and His Father. Beyond all question, the cross speaks of man's antagonism towards Jesus, toward His message, His ideal, His faith and His demand.

And no less clearly this same cross speaks of God's antagonism towards sin. *That* antagonism underlies the severity of the Law, the rites of cleansing, the moral passion of the prophets, the costliness and rigour of the whole sacrificial system, the stern message of John the Baptist. But it stands revealed most clearly in the patient resistance of Jesus to every form of wrong, as He, saddened and alone, goes forth inflexibly to Calvary rather than compromise with evil, excuse hypocrisy, be silent about oppression, abate the truth or dilute the divine demand.

Yet out of the vortex of this double antagonism that swirls about the cross — men's antagonism towards Christ and God's toward sin — there is achieved the miracle of reconciliation: men and God that same day are made friends together. Not that God needed to be reconciled, the enmity, suspicion, resentment are in the hearts of men toward their Maker. But the love of Christ at Calvary dissolves the suspicion, allays the bitterness, answers the accusations that God does not care. The cross is the antidote to all that poisons man's thought about God, and man and God may be at one again. Men may look up in trust and call God Father; God looks down in mercy, calling men His sons.

Just because at Calvary sin is exposed and dealt with, dragged into the daylight of history and purged upon the altars of eternity, man is reconciled to God, and so to *himself, to life* and to his *destiny.* Estrangement is over, the arms of the cross stretch east and west to bind the world together, and up and down to symbolise the meeting place where mercy and truth are met together, righteousness and peace have kissed each other. The nail-scarred hand of Jesus has clasped the soiled hand of sinful man and placed it firmly into the hand of God. What is the reconciliation of Pilate and Herod beside this? For this is the message of true friendship that sounds across the hills above Jerusalem under the darkened skies: Glory be to God in the highest, and on earth peace, goodwill towards men. For God was in Christ, reconciling the world unto Himself.

21 The Barriers Go Down

*"And, behold, the veil of the temple was rent in twain from the
top to the bottom."*
*"Christ is not entered into the holy places made with hands . . .
but into heaven itself."*

Matthew 27:51, Hebrews 9:24

THE RENDING of the rich hanging curtain which screened the holiest shrine in the Jewish Temple was apparently only a minor consequence of the earthquake which rocked Jerusalem as the drama
of the crucifixion reached its climax. The Jew-in-the-street might
see nothing of special interest in the event. But Christians saw in
it a significance, even a symbolism, closely linked to the meaning
of Jesus' death. Early Jewish Christians, indeed, might have said
—with very much of truth — that Christ died *in order that* the
veil might thus be rent, for ever.

To appreciate this symbolism, it is necessary to think in terms
of Hebrew faith, and especially of the priestly code. In that context of thought, the destruction of the sacred curtain meant two
things: the final removal of all barriers between man and God;
and the ultimate fulfilment of the ancient priestly rites, which
could now therefore pass away. In both respects, the rending of
the veil marked the end of an epoch, the beginning of a new dis-
pensation, a total revolution in divine-human relationships. No
"iron curtain" of modern day could constitute a barrier more
formidable, or more rigid, than that double curtain of richly em-
broidered fabric that marked the limit of the public courts within
the Temple and guarded the sanctity of the Holy of Holies.

Its function was, in part, to *hide*. Secrecy was part of much
ancient religion: the gods kept their privacy; the inner mysteries
were only for the "initiates", the favoured, and the priests. Even
in Israel this secrecy was emphasised. The Most Holy Place stood
within a series of courts: the outermost for Gentiles, the next for
women, the next for men, the inner one for priests, the inmost
barred to all but the High Priest himself. At each step, mystery
and darkness deepened. The outward areas enjoyed the daylight;

100

the Holy Place was shadowed, save for the light of the great golden candlestick; the inmost shrine lay in total darkness, empty, secret. God was unknowable: none might see Him and live.

But the rending of the veil *let in the light*; "the darkness is passed, the true light now shineth. . . . The Son of God is come and hath given us an understanding, that we may know him that is true". So John proclaims: though no man might see God at any time "the only begotten Son, which was in the bosom of the father, he hath declared him". The secret is out: God has been made known. His heart stands fully revealed.

For upon the cross the redeeming love of the eternal is made perfectly plain. Now, if anything be hid, it is hid to them that are lost: "for the light of the knowledge of the glory of God hath shined in our hearts". Whereas in olden days, clouds and darkness were round about the throne, and the Lord spoke unto Moses out of thick darkness, in the New Testament the Lord is the light of the Holy City, and about the throne is a rainbow of glorious promise. "The veil," says Paul, "is *done away* in Christ".

But the veil was intended also to *exclude*. Only the High Priest might pass its folds, and he only once a year, to sprinkle on the mercy-seat the blood of the atoning sacrifice and to intercede for the sins of Israel. The great laver for washing, the altar of burnt offering, cords and bars and thresholds threatening death to any who passed beyond their appointed limit — all emphasised that God was *unapproachable*. Sacrifice and priesthood underlined the need for *mediation*: and kept the common folk at a respectful distance from the Most High, and the Most Holy.

But the veil was rent, by God Himself, "from the top", at the death of Jesus, and the way into the holiest was "made manifest". The rending of the veil *let in the worshipper*. Henceforth, we may "come boldly to the throne of grace, to obtain mercy and find grace to help in time of need". "Having therefore, brethren, boldness to enter into the holiest by the blood of Jesus, by a new and living way which he hath consecrated for us . . . let us draw near with full assurance of faith."

For the gospel proclaims the barriers are down: the way to God is open. "We have access," cries Paul again and again, as though his Jewish heart could not believe his ears! "We have access, by one Spirit unto the Father"; "we have access into this grace wherein we stand"; "in him we have boldness, and access with confidence." For the veil is rent and the worshipper is welcome, and we are *all* priests unto God, the Father. The Unknowable is known, and the Unapproachable grants audience, for the veil of the Temple is rent in twain.

This much is clear. But when we ask on what grounds this rending of the ancient veil is possible — that sinful, darkened souls may freely approach the everlasting Light — we enter, indeed, the Holy Place of Scripture, and do well to come unshod, with reverent and humble mind. For the veil was rent, we venture to say, not only to let in the light, and the worshipper, but *to let in the Lord.* "Christ is not entered into the holy places made with hands . . . but into heaven itself", having "an unchangeable priesthood"; "by his own blood he entered in once into the Holy Place having obtained eternal redemption for us", and there He "appears in the presence of God for us".

This profound conception of Christ as High Priest of humanity, the only Mediator between God and man, the Forerunner within the veil, representing His people at the throne of the most High, carries us to the heart of the meaning of the cross. Here, we may reverently affirm, is the clue to Christ's own moving explanation of His death, the seven sacred words that together enshrine His passion.

So, at least, it would appear. Before the darkness descended upon Calvary, Jesus speaks as Priest, climbing as it were the steps of the altar, approaching God for men. "Father, forgive them" is the *priestly prayer of intercession,* not for them only but for humanity. "This day shalt thou be with me in paradise" is the *priestly pronouncement of pardon,* with assurance of grace and life. "Son, behold thy mother; woman, behold thy son" is, at least in miniature, *the priestly purpose of mediation,* forging fellowship, the ancient conception of priesthood as "bridge building" among men and God.

In the darkness, Jesus appears to speak rather as Sacrifice than Priest: "My God, my God, why hast thou forsaken me" may well be the first words of an ancient lamentation; but on the lips of Jesus they gain immeasurable significance as expressing the supreme consequence of bearing the sin of the world, the loss of the presence of the Father until atonement be complete. If this be indeed the inward aspect of the final Sacrifice for sin, the outward aspect lies in the physical agony, and that seems expressed in the only cry of anguish Jesus uttered — "I thirst".

Then, as the darkness lifted, Jesus speaks again as the returning Priest, charged now to bring the word of a reconciled God to penitent, forgiven men: "It is accomplished" is the declaration of completed work: all is well. "Father, into thy hands I commit my spirit" enshrines the promise of eternal life, and the priestly benediction of a final peace.

Such is the meaning of the cross that appealed to Hebrew minds, schooled in the long tradition of priesthood, mediation, sacrifice, expiation and atonement. Christ our Mediator, Advocate, Priest, "offered himself" — both Priest and Sacrifice — "without spot unto God": and "Having by himself purged our sins sat down on the right hand of the Majesty on high".

For *Him* the veil was rent: for us, too, the new and living way is opened to the presence of God. No man cometh to the Father but by Him, but in Him the ancient types and shadows find their meaning, the solemn rituals are fulfilled and pass away. The barriers are down. The way to the holiest is made manifest, and Jesus "is able to save to the uttermost *all* who come unto God by him seeing he ever liveth to make intercession for them".

Implications that determine character

The commentary of Jesus
The Representative of many
The bondage of freedom
The consecration of life
The secret of overcoming
The compelling motive

22 The Commentary of Jesus

"And now I have told you before it come to pass, that, when it is come to pass, ye might believe."

John 14:29

THE WORDS OF JESUS about His cross are luminous, simple, and of practical intent. However grateful we may be for the teaching of apostles, the insights of theologians and philosophers, poets and expositors, we turn with deeper reverence and attention to the commentary of Christ Himself upon His passion, and we are not disappointed.

Explaining beforehand the suffering that lay ahead, the Master used five simple metaphors, each portraying not His mind only, as He looked toward the cross, but how His death would affect the life and faith of all who followed Him.

The first is the figure of the *road* that He must travel, the path mapped out for Him. "The Son of man indeed goeth as it hath been written of him, but woe to that man by whom the Son of man is betrayed!" The way ahead is hard, though clear: it leads directly uphill to the cross. But Jesus has no doubt it is the way appointed, and He sets His face "flintwise", as Luke says, to follow it.

Here at the outset is denial of any mere tragedy, or miscarriage of God's plan. "Ought not the Christ to suffer these things . . . that repentance and remission of sins might be preached in his name? And beginning at Moses and the prophets he expounded unto them in all the scriptures the things concerning himself." This Via Dolorosa was the race set before Him, and He ran it with patience, enduring the cross and despising the shame, because "this commandment have I received of my father".

Yet many contributed to make that way painful to His feet. Judas and Pilate and Caiaphas and the crowds, with Peter too, and Pharisee hecklers and false witnesses and unnecessarily cruel soldiers out for sport. All added their flints, made the road steeper, shaped the way of pain; and for their several parts will bear their woe. But none-the-less the way is the way of the Father's appointment, and He treads it firmly with obedience and courage.

One remembers here the noble words of Joseph to his brethren: "Be not distressed and angry with yourselves because ye sold me here, for it was not you who sent me here, but God". That insight, faith and courage, seeing behind the evil that men do the over-riding will of God shaping our experience, is essential to all who tread the road with Jesus. "The Son of man goeth. . . . Follow me!"

The second figure which Jesus applies to His passion is that of the *cup*: Ye shall indeed drink of the cup that I drink of". Seventeen out of twenty times in the Old Testament this metaphor refers to a cup of divinely appointed suffering — not man's shaping at all now, but God's. "The cup which my Father hath appointed me to drink, shall I not drink it? . . . Father, if it be possible, let this cup pass from me; nevertheless, not my will but thine be done."

The root idea is not easy to define: some think that the cup of God's wrath is implied, or the cup of bitterness which our sins had brewed but which the Father placed into the Saviour's hands. Some think the conception rests on that of the medicinal cup, the bitter draught that heals, or on the ancient poison-cup that tests and purges guilt. Whatever the origin, the meaning is clear: the cup of the world's suffering is drained by Christ, *and we drink it with Him.*

For the Christian cannot insulate himself from the pain and sorrow of humanity. Christ's redemptive pain and atoning death are unique, unsharable; yet we are called to "complete what is lacking in Christ's afflictions for . . . the church". At least that means that we are bound, by His suffering for us, to enter with Him into loving sympathy and vicarious pain with all who suffer; to show a like concern and saving care towards others, as we rejoice to know He showed toward ourselves. The Lord's Supper speaks of many things, but certainly of this, that there is no greatness in His kingdom except as we drink the cup He lifted to His lips.

That thought of greatness, desired and claimed, lies behind the "cup" and also the third figure, that of "the *baptism* I am baptised withal". The expression seems strange until we reflect that the heart of the meaning of baptism lies precisely here, in sharing the cross with Christ. "We are buried with Christ by baptism into death . . . baptised into his death." On the one hand the Old Testament references to "immersion", or being overwhelmed, in adversity lie behind the language: Jesus surrenders to the extremity of suffering, to the limit of death itself. And this, in a degree, we share, as we also die to sin, are crucified with Christ, deny ourselves and take up His cross.

On the other hand, baptism meant for Jewish proselytes, and for John's converts, the beginning of new life. Out of self-judgement and renunciation they rose to glorious new beginnings. Even for Jesus, the cross was initiation into a new life of freedom and triumph: and "as Christ was raised from the dead . . . even so we also should walk in newness of life . . . planted together in the likeness of his resurrection".

Thus for the third time, the language of Jesus implies our participation in His passion. We walk the road of suffering, following Him; we drink the cup of pain, with Him; we are baptised with His baptism. But in the third form of expression there is hope as well as heroism. In dying with Him, we too find gain through loss, triumph through surrender, joy through pain, a fuller, ampler life through taking up the cross and being crucified with Christ.

The fourth and fifth metaphors with which Jesus illumines His death concern rather what He does for us. "Even the Son of man came not to be ministered unto, but to minister, and to give his life a ransom for many." His death is an act of *service*, comparable to washing our feet, healing our wounds, ministering to our sickness. It is something we have to let Him do, gratefully and humbly accepting His service of our need.

How this troubles modern men! And how deep the misunderstanding it exposes! We much prefer to think of Jesus as One to whom we nobly dedicate our all: we will sing for Him around His manger, watch and listen as attentive scholars to His teaching; will fight for Him against all enemies, would wash His wounds, attend His dying. Gladly would we give to Him the service of our lives, our loyalty and strength, our thought and love. Our chief complaint is that we can achieve so little for His glory.

Sharply across all our strong, sincere profession cuts His word:

"The Son of man did not come to be served . . . but to serve", not that we might do our utmost for Him, but that He might do all for us. Until we let Him serve us, no service of ours can matter to Him: "Except I wash thee, thou hast no part with me". We strive so hard to deserve His pardon, to be worthy of acceptance, and find it humbling to have to acknowledge that without Him we can do nothing. Yet until we realise our need, acknowledge our inability to ransom ourselves, humbly and penitently receive Him as our *necessary* Saviour, His cross means nothing to us.

And so His fifth and final word about His death assures us that He is sufficient, dependable and sure. "This cup is the cup of a new *covenant* in my blood." As He is about to leave them, He pledges them in all solemnity to leave them never; as He appears to move towards defeat, He covenants with them to meet and drink with them in the triumph of the kingdom. The love they have known in Him shall not be broken, the grace they have felt through Him shall not fail: He pledges them that He will see them through whatsoever the future holds. His death for them shall seal the compact which neither time nor eternity shall end.

Doubtless behind this metaphor also lies a history of deep thought. The ancient mingling of blood to seal a covenant of friendship, the bedrock covenant of God with Abraham, renewed with Moses, revised with Jeremiah, and now established in Jesus, forms the deepest foundation of all the redeeming work which brings Jesus now to Calvary. But as under the shadow of the cross He bids them drink together, it is of this binding betrothal of His soul to theirs and theirs to Him in unbreakable fealty that He speaks. And were it not for this assurance of His faithfulness, the road, the cup, the baptism would be beyond our powers.

23 The Representative of Many

The Son of man came . . . to give his life a ransom for many."
"By the obedience of one shall many be made righteous."

Matthew 20:28, Romans 5:19

THE INTENSE LONELINESS of Jesus, in His consecration, in His conflict, and in His passion, is somehow emphasised by the thronging crowds who follow Him at the beginning of the story and at its end.

At the beginning, the inn is too full to offer Him hospitality, Jerusalem too crowded for His parents to find Him easily. Galilee provides a multitude wherever He preaches, and men cannot come at Him for the press. One seeks to touch Him while remaining hidden in the throng, and so many crowd upon Him that He must remain in open places, and "they come to him from every quarter". He has no leisure so much as to eat. A vast concourse partake of His bounty and would make Him King by force — and at Ilis refusal begin to melt away. His ministry began in a blaze of popularity.

At the end, the crowds return. A multitude accompanies Him through Jericho, and flock to Bethany to see Lazarus. Jesus rides amid long trains of pilgrims to a city overflowing for the Passover, and the Temple courts are crowded for His last addresses. So great is the popular excitement that the priests at first postpone action against Jesus, fearing the people. When during hours of darkness they take the risk of arresting Jesus, the crowd is there in the morning to shout, "Crucify him", and remains to revile at the foot of the cross. His life ended, too, before the gaze of the multitude.

The crowds are there, at beginning and at end, and yet He walks alone — so little understood, His vision so little comprehended, His suffering so little shared. He is left alone to pray beneath the trees in sad Gethsemane, and completely alone at last when all forsake and flee. He is the lonely *One*, yet in Him *many* find salvation.

This strange bond and contrast between the One and the many

111

is expressed in most of the great words about the cross. "He came to give his life a ransom for many", "by the obedience of one many shall be made righteous." "He hath borne our griefs and carried our sorrows"; "He was wounded for our transgressions"; "*all* we like sheep have gone astray"; "the Lord hath laid on *him* the iniquity of us all." "For the transgression of my *people* was *he* stricken." "By his knowledge shall my righteous servant justify many"; "He bare the sin of many." Always there is recalled this relationship of one Servant, one Saviour, one Sacrifice, and many healed, justified, saved. "One died for all."

In one sense, of course, there is something here common to human life, and it must not be overlooked. *No* man liveth to himself, or dieth to himself. We are "bound in the bundle of life" with many, and self-isolation is not only folly, but a lie. At birth, in life, and in death we are part of the race: no man is an island. The one and the many belong together in the nature of things.

But there is more here than this. There is the special substitutionary-representative character of all the great ones of the earth, of all the outstanding figures who do the crowd's thinking for them as original teachers and prophets; who represent the crowd's cause and conscience, as pioneers and reformers of society; who in days of peril embody the crowd's resistance, as some great war-leader; who express the popular will and desire, as do great actors, poets and heroes; who bear the suffering and pain that must be borne, often at the crowd's hands yet for the crowd's sake, as martyrs and saints. All such are lonely figures, who pass among the crowd unacknowledged sometimes, or dishonoured, yet serving the many by their loneliness, their toil, their pain.

Is all this far below the work of that one Servant who shall justify many, that one Sacrifice for sin who died for all? It is indeed, yet of the same *kind* surely. *Substitution,* by which one soul enters into another's pain and bears another's wrong, that the wrongdoer might go free, and *representation,* by which one soul thinks and does and suffers on behalf of others what by his example they come to think and do and suffer for themselves — this wonderful relationship by which lives are bound together in love and gracious deeds of mercy, is of the very essence of the moral life, the heart of all saintliness, the very stuff of heroism.

112

To call it "immoral" is sheer paradox. It would be an infinitely poorer world if every man bore only his own burden, and none stood out, above and apart from the crowd, to do and suffer what the crowd does not yet understand, but will one day thank God for.

Parents, partners, leaders, saints, thinkers, missionaries, priests, and martyrs all in their varied ways exhibit the grace of vicarious service, suffering *instead* of others as their substitute, striving *on behalf of* others as their representative. And what is it all but the pale reflection of the divine principle of redemption: One for many, bearing their sins, paying their debts, dying for all? Jesus passes lonely amidst the crowds because, while one with them He yet is different — their Substitute-Representative.

Of the two sides, or halves, of this truth, the former is by far the more familiar. It lies in Jesus' phrase about giving His life a ransom *instead of* many, and behind the whole metaphor of debt, and the One who paid the debt to set us free. It is implied even more clearly in the whole institution of sacrifice, and in the use of sacrificial language to interpret Christ's passion. Jesus is the sinner's "stand-in", doing for us all what we have no resources, or strength, or will to do for ourselves.

Much less familiar is the thought of Jesus as our Representative. Yet that is equally plainly part of New Testament teaching, and without it the idea of substitution *can* be crudely exaggerated in immoral ways. "He died *on behalf of* us all" is the more frequent scriptural formulation of the relation of His death to the many who are saved. And what is done "on behalf of" others, they are bound to ratify, confirm, acknowledge as done *in their name* and done *by them*.

This is the basic meaning of the title Advocate which John applies to Jesus, and it is the precious truth that underlies the glorious High Priestly ministry which Jesus exercises for His own. Christ is entered into heaven itself, now to appear in the presence of God on our behalf, ever living to make intercession for us. The idea of representation of others is as essential to His priesthood, as the idea of substitution for others is essential to His sacrifice. And the two belong together: to conceive them always together would save many a fruitless argument about the meaning of the cross.

113

And many a fruitless life. For the truth of Christ's representation of us all at Calvary is vital for sound faith and fruitful character. Jesus is the new Adam, Head and Representative of a new humanity; He died for all, and in Him we die. This Paul plainly argues with the most practical intent. "We thus judge, that if one died for all, *then were all dead* . . ." — that is representation. It means that we accept what Jesus did for us: His judgement on our sin, His renunciation as our renunciation, His utter repudiation of evil as our own. We are crucified with Christ, buried with Christ, risen with Christ, as Christian baptism vividly declares. We too die, to sin, to the flesh, to the world.

This is the moral safeguard of a gospel of free salvation through the "finished work" of Christ. The power of that gospel to change sinners has not always been in evidence precisely because we have obscured identification with Jesus in His death as a vital part of saving faith.

Is not this why Jesus took elaborate pains to get alone, and undisturbed, with His disciples to prepare them for the end; and why He bade them take into their own hands bread, and wine, to make their own the meaning of His passion? He took them to the garden, would have them stay awake, witness His arrest, and pray lest they too enter testing. He had said, as plainly as words allow, that they should drink of His cup and be baptised with His baptism. Indeed, He had declared that unless they took His cross upon themselves they could not be disciples.

In those words the whole meaning and necessity of His work as *representing* many is sharpened to a definite command. We dare not evade it. He died that we might not need to die, eternally; and that we might die with Him. There Christian life begins.

24 *The Bondage of Freedom*

"And when they had bound Jesus they led him away. . . . Then released he Barabbas unto them."
"And so Pilate . . . released Barabbas . . . and delivered Jesus to be crucified."
"And he released unto them . . . whom they had desired; but he delivered Jesus to their will."
Let these go their way. . . . [they] took Jesus, and bound him, and led him away."
"God sent forth his Son, . . . made under the law, to redeem them that are under the law."

Matthew 27:2, 26, Mark 15:15, Luke 23:25,
John 18:8, 12, 13, Galatians 4:4, 5.

IT IS NOT SURPRISING that the New Testament should repeatedly set side by side the freedom that came to Barabbas and the fetters fastened upon Jesus, the escape of the disciples and the arrest of their Master, the subjection of Jesus to the law and the setting free of them that were under the law. For very much of the meaning of the cross may be set forth in the language of bondage and freedom, though the truth conveyed is not quite so obvious as at first appears.

Christianity is essentially redemptive; probably the best loved of all Christ's names is the name "Redeemer". The breath of freedom is in that word. Behind it, in the thought of every Jew, lay the story of the exodus from the land of bitterness and hard bondage into the freedom of the land of promise. Around it, in the first century, lay the institution of slavery, and the rules for "redemption" of the purchased servant. News of a Redeemer spoke straight to the heart of Jew and pagan alike, offering men freedom. All unconsciously, Barabbas found what countless thousands were later to discover, that the dying Christ proclaimed liberty to captives, the opening of the prison to them that were bound.

But the release of Barabbas involved delivering Jesus to be crucified. Our redemption implies His bondage — His fetters set us free. But it was not men alone who bound Him: His love for men that made Him come to seek that which was lost, and give His life a ransom for many — *that* bound His soul to the horns of the altar. His obedience to the Father, who gave Him commandment, appointing Him the cup to drink and the baptism to be baptised withal, before whose will in Gethsemane His own will instantly bowed — *that* bound His soul to the cross men made for Him. And His own steadfast character, as the Good Shepherd giving His life for the sheep, the Saviour working the works of Him who sent Him, the dauntless Messiah steadfastly setting His face towards Jerusalem — *that* equally bound Him to His saving purpose. "The Son of man must suffer . . ." — there lies the inner bondage by which mankind was freed.

Paul traces that inner constraint back to its source when he says that in order to purchase the freedom of men under the curse of the law Jesus was Himself born under the law, accepting for our sakes all the human discipline of obedience and the responsibilities of our failure. So emptying Himself He took the form of a servant, was made in the likeness of men and became obedient unto death. Men bound Him at His trial and to His cross, but they could not bind Him more securely than He was already bound by His own love, obedience and will to save.

Because He consented to captivity, the disciples had opportunity to escape: because He is bound, Barabbas is free. Here is a key-note of the gospel of redemption, and within it the two ideas of bondage and freedom sound closely together. Our sore bondage needed His willing bondage to set us free. The freedom wherewith Christ has made us free is a large freedom, touching many sides of life. It includes freedom from sin's ultimate penalties, in the pardon of God: and it liberates as much from the hold and fascination of sin, as from its consequences. It is freedom from fear, too, freedom from the fear of life and of God that can paralyse the will and make faith and hope impossible. It is freedom for those whose consciences have been fettered and imprisoned in a system of laws and rules that make godliness a burden and doing right a drudgery, the freedom to which Augustine refers in the famous counsel: "Love God and do what you will". Freedom in Christ is the liberty to break with tradition where tradition stultifies the truth — being redeemed from vain conversation received by tradition from the fathers. It is freedom from the daily harassing care that binds the soul to little things and narrows life down to merely making ends meet. And at the last it is freedom from the very bondage of corruption into the liberty of life eternal.

It is a glorious prospect, this freedom of the Christian man. To say with the Jews of Christ's day, "We were never in bondage", is merely to betray that the fetters have become too familiar to be felt. "If the Son shall make you free, ye shall be free indeed."

And He does. He brings the truth which makes free in the realm of the mind, and the sacrifice of His blood, which redeems the soul, and the assurance of love which liberates the heart, the rule of the Spirit of life which makes free from the rule of sin and death.

And yet there is bondage. Christian liberty is not license. As the freedom of Barabbas involved the bondage of Christ, and the redemption of the world implied the obedience of the Servant of the Lord, so our spiritual freedom has at the heart of it a new and willing bondage. Paul delights to call himself the bondslave of Christ, and he does not hesitate to speak of slave-masters as having their Master in heaven, and of slaves as freemen, though servants of Christ.

Peter too reminds his readers that they are "free, yet . . . servants" or slaves to God. Possibly he remembered how the crowds turned back in Galilee, and Jesus asked the disciples sadly, "Will ye also go away?" Then Peter had answered for the rest, "Lord, to whom shall we go? Thou hast the words of eternal life", well knowing even then that Christ had enslaved them by the very love that set them free. There came a time when Peter with curses declared himself free of Jesus, free of His claims, His friendship and His memory. But Peter afterwards remembered the bitter tears which that asserted freedom cost, and knew himself bound more closely than ever: "Lord, thou knowest all things, thou knowest that I love thee".

"All things are yours," says Paul: that is the Christian's freedom to have, and use, and enjoy, and profit. "And ye are Christ's": that is the Christian's bondage. "Ye are not your own, ye are bought. . . ." The love that frees us is the love which now constrains to the service which is perfect freedom.

Human nature is never at its best, never really happy, in its wild, undisciplined state. Unchartered freedom wearies, and finally destroys; man at his noblest, as Chesterton argued, is man making vows and binding himself by great oaths. But the highest human bondage is the bondage of love, self-accepted, motivated by delight and gratitude, expressing itself in glad free loyalty and devotion. And such is the bondage of Christ.

The most penetrating thing ever written about man's redemption is that saying of Paul, looking backwards to the exodus and forwards to the glory, that God "hath *delivered* us from the power of darkness, and hath translated us into the *kingdom* of the Son of his love." Out of the bondage of sin, into the bondage of Christ: that is redemption. It is ours, because Christ consented to be bound.

In the days of early discipleship, we are possessed by the sense of our new-found freedom: liberty is our watchword and our song. As we mature, the liberty grows no whit less wonderful, but the bondage grows more firm: we love Him because He first loved us, we know we are henceforth, else sinning greatly, dedicated spirits.

According to Hebrew law, a slave who had served his Master for six years was freed in the seventh, unless he freely chose to remain in service. Then his master took him to the doorpost and pierced his ear in token of life-long devotion, the slave saying meanwhile, "I love my Master, I will not go out free". So the writer of the fortieth Psalm declares, "I delight to do thy will, O God . . . . Mine ears hast thou pierced". And so, too, Frances Ridley Havergal sings:

> *I love, I love my Master,*
> *I will not go out free!*
> *For He is my Redeemer,*
> *He paid the price for me.*
> *I will not leave His service,*
> *It is so sweet and blest;*
> *And in the weariest moments*
> *He gives the truest rest —*
> *Rejoicing and adoring,*
> *Henceforth my song shall be,*
> *"I love, I love my Master,*
> *I will not go out free!"*

That is the bondage which makes us truly free.

25 The Consecration of Life

"The Son of man came . . . to give his life."
"For their sakes I sanctify myself."
"I lay down my life."

Mark 10:45, John 17:19; 10:17

"GOD HATH GIVEN to us eternal life, and this life is in his Son. . . . I am come that they might have life, and have it more abundantly." The emphasis of the Christian gospel upon fullness and richness of life is unique among the world's religions, which are more often absorbed in negative and life-renouncing attitudes than in the positive enjoyment of life in God. The gift of Christ is eternal life, not simply in the sense that life shall last forever, but in the deeper sense that it shall be worthy of lasting, as partaking already of eternal quality and value. It is life abundant, victorious, enriched, and rejoicing, and it draws its fullness of strength and of worth from God, from whom it is derived and to whom it returns in consecration.

It is well to give careful thought to this positive message of the gospel as we stand beneath the cross, because there our minds turn more easily towards ideas of death, renunciation, sacrifice. Yet the message of the passion is not of death only, but of life, life given, sanctified, laid down, as the source of our life and the pattern for its consecration.

"The Son of man came . . . to *give* his life", and we miss something of the wonder of the gift if we think *only* of His death. He gave Himself unstintedly for us, before He gave Himself finally in His passion; all the way from glory back to glory He emptied Himself, pouring out His soul, spending Himself for us. The manner of His death but crowned the manner of His life, and in this gift of life lies part of the meaning of true consecration.

The Gospels are full of busy, hurrying figures: fishers, sowers, stewards, husbandmen, users of talents, investors, people clothing the naked, feeding the hungry, visiting the prisoner, tending the sick, making bread, building towers, searching for lost things, bending over the wounded, attending the sick, travelling, cleaning

119

rooms, digging, and many, many other useful, active, toiling folk. Not a monk, a student, or an idler appears: in Christ's world there is much to do. "Go, work today in my vineyard" is His command; "What *do* ye?" is His question; "Cut it down, why cumbereth it the ground?" is His comment upon the unproductive. For to Christ's mind, life is for use, and there is no consecration of life without activity, service and toil.

This prodigal use of life is not only central to Christ's demand of us, but it is, He says, the way to fuller life. "He that saveth his life" — hoarding it jealously to himself for his own purposes and enjoyment — "shall lose it: he that loseth his life" — spending it freely, pouring it out "for my sake and the gospel's" — "the same shall save it." We usually understand this as a promise: rather it is a law, a statement of fact. Those who live for themselves do in practice reach a point where they ask what there is to live for: they who have learned of Christ to give life away, in time, strength, friendship, love and service, live to the full, and live ever gratefully.

"For their sakes, I sanctify myself." This is the second element in life's consecration, and for many, the most difficult. It involves life's dedication *exclusively* to God's will, as Christ Himself was "set apart" for the work to which He was appointed. "Sanctification", for some minds, is but one step removed from "sanctimonious"; for others it savours of something puritanical — and our generation has a morbid phobia concerning "narrowness".

Few will deny the danger of exaggeration: but the truth remains. Jesus was no ascetic, but His rule for fulness of life is plain. "Enter ye in at the narrow gate; for wide is the gate and broad is the way, that leadeth to destruction, and the crowds walk thereupon. But narrow is the gate, straitened is the way, that *leadeth unto life* — and few there are that find it!" There is a breadth which makes for shallowness, and mud; there is a narrowness which keeps the current of life swift and strong and clean.

Why should we be so fearful of it? Without narrowness there can be no lasting friendship — but then we call it loyalty. Without it there can be no intense thought, or study — but then we call it concentration. Without it there can certainly be no character — but then we call it discipline. Without it there can be no great career, no proficiency, no research, but in these realms we rename narrowness application, training, specialisation, and realise its value. Mortals just cannot be, or do, everything; if we set out to follow all the stars we shall end surely in the ditch.

Life must be narrowed down to reasonably limited objectives, if we are to get anywhere, and no life can hope to achieve greatness until it is so focussed, disciplined, dedicated. Is it then unreasonable, or unsafe, to counsel a similar *concentration* in the Christian life — a determination to do at least this one thing properly, to follow Christ? The aim, and the result, is not less of life but more and richer, as the Master says. And His word is reinforced for us by the contemporary situation.

"We live," said a President of Methodist Conference recently, "in an age of tattered morals", and we can all supply the evidence that supports the melancholy judgement. "We live," say other leaders of religious life, "in the ebb-tide of the Spirit, when Christian work is beset by problems and bereft of power." The only adequate answer to both needs is a greater appreciation of the worth of *holiness;* a genuine and gracious puritanism that is all the more conscientious about truth, purity, honesty and good faith because the world is forgetting what these things mean; and a true and humble sanctification which will liberate once more amongst us the power of God's Holy Spirit.

But how far should we go in life-spending and in dedication? To what lengths is such consecration really required of us? In one sense the answer has got to be our own. "No man taketh my life from me," said Jesus, but He added, "*I lay it down* of myself." We must draw our own limits of self-giving, tenderness of conscience, holy living and self-denial: but we do it beneath the cross, where He drew none.

Inevitably in a century like ours the deep desire of multitudes is for social security, making every provision that foresight and ingenuity can suggest against emergencies. Most of us ardently desire a safe job, a worthwhile career, a sure foothold in the world, a bomb-proof shelter if the worst should come, a reserve of capital, a protected home and family circle to which to retreat from the hazards of the world. It is a worthy desire, and for it many are willing to work hard and to make sacrifice. And some remember that, these things being achieved, something should be left for God.

In this atmosphere of our time it is hard to hear Jesus say, "I lay down my life", and to remember it meant for Him turning away deliberately from such security, such ordinary quietness and sheltered peace as Nazareth offered Him. But so it did: He went forth from just such an ivory-tower of village life to face the crowds, endure the contradiction of sinners against Himself, challenge the half-truth and the wrong, outface hypocrisy, set His face as flint to go to Jerusalem, tread the Via Dolorosa and accept the cross. He at least, willingly, and for our sakes, went the whole way in consecration. For Him self-giving and sanctification led on to sacrifice.

Whatever our modern desire for security, the call of Jesus to follow Him remains as challenging and as clear as ever. Some have followed through conflict to martyrdom; some through years of costly toil, and missionary pioneering. Some have made heavy sacrifices for honesty, truth, or service of others. In some lands still the ultimate sacrifice may be demanded.

And His right to call us so, remains unchallenged. He lay down His life for us: we ought to lay down our lives for Him and for the brethren.

> Oh, let my life be given,
>   My years for Thee be spent,
> World-fetters all be riven,
>   And joy with suffering blent:
> Thou gav'st Thyself for me;
>   I give myself to Thee!

26 The Secret of Overcoming

"Be of good cheer; I have overcome the world."
*"They overcame him by the blood of the Lamb, and by the word
of their testimony; and they loved not their lives unto the death."*

John 16:33, Revelation 12:11

EVERYTHING IN THE BOOK of Revelation is to be understood against
the background of intense conflict. It is an underground pam-
phlet, secretly circulated to trusted friends, a handbook of Christian
resistance to Roman oppression, with many pointed allusions to
those in authority and to the doom that awaits them. That is why
it is full of the secret signs and hidden symbols, essential in a book
whose very possession might mean death.

The undertone of the whole prophecy is a call to arms. Echo-
ing throughout its pages are the cries of the slain and the prayers
of the martyrs. Blood and tears and tension are in every page;
through each glowing paragraph rings the defiant call to resist,
hold fast, be strong, and overcome. For the future is sure, the
end is in sight, Christ shall conquer Caesar, the church shall out-
last the State, faith shall vanquish the sword, and mighty Rome
shall fall in ruins in the great and terrible "Day of the Lord".

Rome has changed her policy since Paul appealed to Caesar: by
ostracism, fines, threats, imprisonment, death, a policy of suppres-
sion is being pursued throughout the Empire, and everywhere
priests of the Caesar-cult inform against the Christians. Yet this
main struggle with the State has but thrown into sharper relief
the ceaseless warfare of the Christian upon other fronts.

Always surrounding that infant church stood the brazen entice-
ments of a luxurious and often vicious paganism. Theatres, tem-
ples, clubs and festivals full of uncleanness and cruelty presented
a constant challenge to newly-won converts struggling to keep
themselves unspotted from the world. Within the churches, the
struggle seemed unequal, defeat certain, the cost of loyalty so high,
that none can blame if Sardis, Ephesus, Pergamos, Laodicea grew
slack and cool and ready to compromise.

For the leaders and their loved ones, there was the ever-present

123

threat of death, the constant struggle to conquer fear and face
with victorious faith a martyr-death and the unknown beyond.
Thus did it seem, to those scattered communities of Asia Minor,
that they were called upon to fight upon four fronts at once: and
the pressure was hard.

To these tiny churches, engaged thus in so cruel and so crucial
a warfare, this wonderful book is sent, from one himself in puni-
tive exile, to stiffen resistance, to rouse to heroism, to nerve for
victory, to fortify with a great faith, and to comfort with an undying hope. And not least to celebrate with a flourish of trumpets
the lengthening roll of those who had been faithful unto death,
resisting unto blood, the undefeated who suffer no more because
by way of blood and fire they have passed to where beyond these
conflicts there is peace.

This is their epitaph: "They overcame . . . by the blood of the
Lamb, and by the word of their testimony; and they loved not their
lives unto the death". This was the threefold secret of their
victory, as it is of ours. For still the rival powers contend, man's
rule challenging God's, the world opposing the church, worldliness,
weakness and fear in conflict with the patience of the saints. Still
are we called to fight and conquer, to wrestle and to overcome,
and we shall do neither save as they did long ago: by the blood
of the Lamb, the word of testimony, and the loyalty that loves not
its own life unto the end.

"The blood of the Lamb" is one of those great New Testament phrases whose meaning bursts the bounds of language. Originally it signified that Jesus died as sacrifice for the sins of the
world, the Lamb slain for our redemption, His blood shed for remission of sins, His life offered in final atonement for a world under judgement. But the phrase comes to gather up within itself
the whole *fact* of Calvary: of the exposure of sin's nature and
seriousness such atonement implies; of Christ's unrelenting resistance towards evil; of His example of submission to the Father's
will; of His wresting triumph from the worst His enemies could
do, and carrying off their crown of thorns, their mocking purple,
the very gibbet they framed for Him, to be the insignia of His
coronation in a million hearts.

This stupendous fact, that Jesus opposed sin with His life, died

resisting violence, lies, oppression, hatred for our sakes, died hero-
ically, undefeated — this is the signal for Christian revolt against
the lies and lusts and lovelessness that threatens to destroy man's
soul. Pagan religion, and even pagan ethics, issued no such call
to moral heroism, or resistance against evil. But the death of Jesus
left no doubt where Christians stand: the enemy is sin within the
heart, the Christian is committed to resolute and uncompromising
opposition, and to believe that though goodness suffer, it shall
conquer in the end.

And behind this faith is the assurance — in the blood of the
Lamb — that God is not aloof from the struggle, unmoved, waiting
only the final round and ultimate judgment. He knows, and feels
and cares; He suffers in the humanity He fashioned, is in the conflict with us. He is not to be dreaded, though our hearts be guilty,
but to be trusted, not waiting to be angry, but reconciled, not
against us but on our side. So stands the cross, towering above our
changing moods, unshaken with the convulsions of time, branded
indelibly into history, declaring for all time God's resistance to sin
and God's love to sinners. That fact is the very standing ground
of Christian victory.

Yet such a fact, even so significant a fact, is something still ex-
ternal to ourselves, until its meaning be accepted, its power acknowledged, within the soul. Upon the historic fact that Jesus died
for men, must rest the personal faith that knows He died for me,
and so the fact of Calvary becomes an *experience* of redeeming
love. To hearts that so believe come peace, and free forgiveness,
the cleansing and renewal of the soul, the joy of fellowship with a
reconciled God, the high impulse of a great gratitude that knows
itself unpayably indebted to God's mercy. Within the heart that
once has rested at the foot of Christ's cross, all manner of motives,
powers and high ideals are kindled: from that place of death new
life streams forth to every soul who trusts.

This was the testimony of those who fought and suffered beneath the banner of the cross. They preached Christ crucified, the
wisdom and the power of God, because they found Him so. They
knew themselves comforted, strengthened, set free, ennobled, disciplined and constrained by all that Christ had done for them. In
a world of slipping standards, beset with innumerable temptations
to sin and to despair, they felt themselves upheld, by gratitude

and love and hope. Their faith in Him who died, and their experience of His keeping power, was the very life-line of their victory.

One thing more remains. As the fact, through faith, became experience, so the experience, by its powerful moral constraint, became their *standard*. They too, in turn, loved not their lives unto the death. The point is quite crucial to Christian overcoming. The acceptance of the cross is no less essential to Christian victory than is knowledge of Christ's passion, or faith in His redeeming grace.

For it is not our hopes, dreams, ambitions, that are promised victory: nor that we shall receive all we desire, our every prayer granted, the things we fear all taken from us. As we are schooled more and more to obedience, even that might come to pass for us. But the assurance in which we fight is that His plans shall succeed, His cause prosper, His truth prevail — not ours. Beneath the cross we learn that victory lies within submission.

Thus all He did becomes the standard and the ruling passion of those that draw their strength from Him. He that loveth his life shall lose it: he that loseth his life for Christ's sake and the gospel's the same shall save it. We are not made to triumph, rather are we led in the train of His triumph; we overcome in just that measure in which He first has overcome our hearts. Those who are thus content that He should win, achieve a wonderful immunity from the stress and wounds and fears of this world's strife. They truly conquer by capitulation, and overcome by loving not their own lives to the end, as did their Lord.

> *Make me a captive, Lord,*
> *And then I shall be free*
> *Force me to render up my sword*
> *And I shall conqueror be. . . .*
>
> *My will is not my own*
> *Till Thou hast made it Thine;*
> *If it would reach a monarch's throne*
> *It must its crown resign;*
> *It only stands unbent*
> *Amid the clashing strife,*
> *When on Thy bosom it has leant*
> *And found in Thee its life.*

27 The Compelling Motive

"The love of Christ constraineth us."
"We love him, because he first loved us."

II Corinthians 5:14, I John 4:19

A LEADING PSYCHOLOGIST has declared that the major difficulty facing many modern people is not that they are overstrained, but that "they are undermotived". Innate, and almost limitless, resources of spiritual energy are not released because nothing "moves" us deeply enough to call out our powers, or to drive us to the Source of life for spiritual replenishment.

The remark applies with equal force to the average Christian life. We are better equipped intellectually, more articulate, better organised, probably more aware of the social implications of religion, than past generations: but we understand far less how to touch the emotive springs of life, how to operate the inner mechanisms of the soul which, as Americans say, make people "tick". Our greatest campaigns seem mere ripples on the surface of stolid indifference. War, distress, sickness, widespread moral decay, antisocial pressures that threaten to disrupt our civilisation, colossal perils that could easily destroy our world, the fear of hell — none of these things *move* us.

The problem of insufficient emotional incentives is peculiar to our century, and one of its plainest symptoms is boredom. "A purposeless life is a life of fatigue." We seek the stimulus of secondhand emotions artificially evoked by the dream-world of the film, self-created in the excitement of gambling, or portrayed for us in the sex-and-gunsmoke diet of television adjusted to armchairs.

It may be we are too self-analytical to be subject to great emotions. It may be we have had a surfeit of excitement in two world wars. It is certain that religion is the source of life's deepest feelings, and religion has less hold on ours than on previous ages. Whatever the explanation, the lack of moral motive-power is a serious situation for any society.

Paul described the weakness, disunity, darkness of mind, vice, disloyalties, that characterised the Roman world he knew, and added somewhat unexpectedly the penetrating phrase "past feeling", as though to attribute debasement of morals and decay of social well-being to the inability to feel deeply, or be shocked by evil things. A society thus insensitive is free to wander ever further from honour and virtue, until evil no longer impinges upon a general conscience made cynical, hardened, devoid of moral indignation, horror, sympathy, fear, or shame.

Such destruction of moral sensitiveness is the final nemesis upon evil-doing. As Paul would say, "She that liveth in sin is dead while she liveth"; or Robert Burns:

> It petrifies the feeling,
> And hardens a' within.

How insensitive can one get? In twenty-four hours the British government tested its earlier H-bomb, capable of blasting a million people to destruction, and inaugurated its Premium Bonds scheme, the Postmaster-General "picking winners" with an electronic pin. Arranging its News Bulletin for that day, the British Broadcasting Corporation actually placed the gambling item first!

But the deadening result of weakened moral emotions affects the church no less. So many frustrated and despondent Christians, lacking radiance, so dull familiarity with sacred things, so much earnest debate and intellectual ferment with so little *done*, all reveals that Christians too can get "past feeling". The need is certainly not for more emotional outbursts of undirected energy, but how we all long for the steady, enduring flame of spiritual passion that glows brightest when the world is chill, something to kindle, bestir, inspire, flare up with radiance, bear us along with singing to great achievement, and *last* until the journey's done!

Paul says he found it — in the cross. The idea that kindled into magnesium light in that profound and argumentative mind was the idea that the Messiah had died to redeem mankind. The spark that fell upon the tinder of that emotional nature and set his soul ablaze was a spark from the torches of those who hunted Jesus through the dark streets of Jerusalem on the night on which He was betrayed. The invisible finger that touched to life the vital spot where his secret self lay bound, was the finger of a pierced hand. The *suffering of Jesus* was the key that unleashed the forces of that gigantic personality: 'I live by the faith of the Son of God, who loved me and gave himself for me. . . . The love of Christ *constraineth* me".

Do we appear to be beside ourselves? then this is why: Christ, Christ's love, Christ's *dying* love, has laid hold of us, "controls us", has become the innermost compulsion of our being. We are uplifted, upheld, carried in triumph, by the love of Christ. The love that brought Him to a sinful world, that bared His back for scourging, stretched His hands for nails, bowed His head for thorns, and toiled beneath the cross up the hill of human sin to taste death for every man, has awakened an answering passion in our hearts, humbling and exalting us, shaming and sanctifying, overcoming and overpowering us, constraining us to live for Him alone.

So Paul explains himself. And likewise John: "We love him, because he first loved us". Likewise also — to choose but one out of thousands of later Christians, — the saintly Francis Xavier, whose sixty years of unremitting toil from Italy through India and Malaya to China and Japan lies behind his words:

Thou, O my Jesus, Thou didst me upon the cross embrace;
For me didst bear the nails and spear, and manifold disgrace;
And griefs and torments numberless, and sweat of agony;
E'en death itself — and all for one who was Thine enemy.
Then why, O blessed Jesus Christ, should I not love Thee
*   well?*
Not for the sake of winning heaven, or of escaping hell;
Not with the hope of gaining aught, nor seeking a reward;
But as Thyself hast loved me, O ever-loving Lord.
E'en so I love Thee, and will love, and in Thy praise will sing,
Because Thou art my loving God, and my redeeming King.

No other language satisfies the saints, no other will serve, than this language of love, of passion, of devotion to the person of Jesus. Hero-worship, admiration, idealism focussed upon perfection of example, trust, loyalty, gratitude — especially the last — are all compounded within it. But nothing less than "love" can express what the Christian feels, or meet what Christ demands with His insistent "Lovest thou me?"

Yet the constraining love which moves the Christian heart is no irrational emotion; Paul helps us analyse its power,

It operates, Paul says, *upon the mind*, directing thought into new channels, erecting new standards of comparison, opening new worlds of ideas. "The love of Christ constraineth us, because we thus judge" that His death for us implies our death; that if any man be in Christ he is a new creature; that all things are of God. In the light of the cross all values are transfigured, all souls attain significance, all life is seen as open to redeeming intervention, the supreme tragedy as sin, the supreme folly, despair — since Jesus died for sinners. Thinking motivated by the cross is the wisdom of God.

Constraining love operates, Paul says, *upon the will*, directing into new channels the driving energies of ambition and desire. The life that issued from self, controlled by the impulse to please oneself, justified and applauded by complacent self-approbation, is suddenly diverted, upwards "unto Him", outwards unto others. At the cross where we find ourselves for what we are, we also lose ourselves for what we may become. All great Christian lives show this odd characteristic of selflessness, puzzling and incredible to the non-Christian. They are too humble to think much of themselves, too meek to assert themselves, too grateful to pity themselves, too generous to better themselves at others' expense — yet they get things done. "He died for all, that they which live should not henceforth live unto themselves, but unto him. . . ."

The constraint operates, too, Paul says, *upon the heart*, and operates as love always must, with exclusive power. He must "have the pre-eminence". Body, mind, time, talent, money, strength, life are His, first and only, for love's sake. The heart is made "a new creature", and looks out upon a world where "all things are of God", and feels impelled to break the alabaster of life over His dear feet, and protest through tears of penitence, joy and love, "Lord, thou knowest that I love thee". Such is the authentic reaction of the Christian beneath the cross: in Dora Greenwell's words:

> *It was for me that Jesus died, for me and a world of men*
> *Just as sinful, and just as slow to give back His love again;*
> *And He didn't wait till I came to Him, He loved me at my*
>   *worst,*
> *He needn't ever have died for me if I could have loved Him*
>   *first!*

The Compelling Motive

That is the compelling motive alone sufficient for Christian character, endurance, and service. Within the shadow of His cross the risen Christ, at each memorial Supper, still confronts disciples with the wistful, searching plea, "Lovest thou, *lovest* thou me?"

CONSIDERATIONS THAT ENRICH DEVOTION

The Lord's intention
The signpost of the soul
The focus of remembrance
The Bread of life
The cup of the covenant
The promise of the end

28 The Lord's Intention

"This do ye, as oft. . . ."

I Corinthians 11:25

As A CONGREGATION quietly gathers before the Table of the Lord varied thoughts and feelings take possession of reverent hearts — prayerfulness, thanksgiving, aspiration, regret, and penitence; a new sense of challenge, of consecration, of re-commissioning; memories of the dying Saviour, adoration of the present Lord, a quickening of the advent hope. For some a reminder of new griefs and a whisper of immortality, for others a renewed tenderness of conscience, a fresh promise of victory; these and many other sacred associations are focussed in the memorial service, lending an inexhaustible richness to its meaning. Yet amid all the values which the Lord's Supper enshrines for us, the central, supreme meaning depends upon *our Lord's intention* when He said, "This do . . . . as oft. . ." . And that is neither hard to seek, nor difficult to understand: He meant the commemorative feast for our perpetual comforting.

If that seems an inadequate statement of our Lord's intention, remember that in its original meaning "comfort" is not an emotional term, but a military one, with echoes in it of the ancient word *fortis,* meaning strong, stouthearted; and with other military words — fortify, fortitude — for its near relations. To comfort really means "to increase fortitude" in the heart of another.

Jesus was leaving behind Him, as His only legacy to the world, a group of people, with a new truth in their minds and a great experience in their hearts. But He left no book, no set prescription for worship, discipline, organization, no sheltering institution or school to perpetuate His work. He left simply this fellowship of hearts aflame, indwelt by one Spirit, owning one Name. And for the focal point of that fellowship, He made the recurring appointment to meet together: "This do . . . as oft. . ." .

Out into that ancient world He sent them, to live under God's rule in Caesar's empire, to build His kingdom beneath Caesar's throne, to live Christlike lives in a decaying society, to bear witness in Jerusalem, Judaea, Samaria, unto the uttermost parts of the earth — and to turn the world upside down. And for their need He left them this: bread and wine, and "This do, in remembrance of me". This clearly is His design, that His Table shall ever be the point of perpetual renewal, the still-flowing spring to which the Christian heart repairs to drink again of eternal waters, a kind of altar from whose unquenched flames succeeding generations rekindle their torches and relight their altar-fires. It serves as spiritual armoury wherein the Christian soul may find his helmet and his shield, his breastplate and his sword, and hearing afresh his Captain of Salvation, go forth again to the good fight. It is, too, a place of confession, if we may be allowed a dangerous mataphor, where the stricken heart may sob out its penitence and find again its peace.

Was not *this* our Lord's intention — an oft-recurring means of spiritual renewal, the continual perpetuation of His own ministry projected down the years, constantly rekindling fortitude? He gave it for perpetual comforting.

And how wonderfully this purpose is achieved. The Lord's Supper is essentially something that we share together. To it each turns again from his isolation and loneliness to meet his fellow pilgrims. The Lord's Table becomes a trysting place for friends, a rendezvous for fellow travellers, a rallying point for comrades in a common war.

Here at His Table our individual conversion, private prayers, personal obedience, lonely battles, secret aspirations, are all caught up and linked and interwoven with the same thing in other hearts. It is one bread we break, with the deep undertones of ancient loyalties sealed in the sharing of bread and salt together. It is one cup we drink, with the memory of one people consecrated by sacrifice at Sinai. All that this means in comfort as well as discipline, every practised Christian knows. It does mean discipline, for when our disagreements with others keep us from the Table we know, with an unanswerable inner conviction, that we at least are in the wrong. But it means comfort too: Peter might say, "Though all men forsake, yet will not I" — confident he could stand alone if need be. We know, as he soon knew, that we dare not speak thus. The fellowship of kindred minds is too necessary to our continuance in grace, and so the Lord intended that we oft should come together and strengthen each other's hand in God.

Beside the comfort of renewed companionship, we find the steadying reminder of something once for all accomplished, constant and unchanging. Each Lord's Supper recalls us to that which may be forgotten by the careless, obscured by our unfaithfulness, ignored by the unbelieving, but which cannot be erased, which stands there in history behind us, the constant background of all our lives.

With so many of us, the trouble about steadfast continuance in Christian life is our incessant changeableness, inconstancy of purpose, fluctuating moods. The enthusiasms of youth simmer down, the emotions cease to move so deeply, the clear, unquestioned convictions come to possess a new perspective. Life, and sometimes people, disappoint us, experience may disillusion us, we learn the weakness of our own resolve, the protean forms and resurrection power of our own sins; and many hopes decay.

Of course this is not all the story — it were treachery to suggest it: Yet inconstancy *is* our problem. But

> *When in the maddening maze of things*
> *And tossed by storm and flood*
> *To one fixed trust our spirit clings —*
> *We KNOW that God is good.*

We look out from ourselves, our feelings, our moods, our sins, to one fixed trust: He loved me, and gave Himself for me. The Redeemer's love, and deed, and unswerving purpose to save, enshrined for ever in the historic, unchangeable fact of the cross confront us in the bread and wine, with the deep strong comfort of His finished work. He will not, He cannot deny Himself: and He died for me.

It is but the other side of this to mention the comfort, of an unbroken, and unbreakable, Covenant. This is the Lord's own word for the innermost meaning of His Supper: "This is the cup of a new covenant, in my blood. . ." . The unfamiliar, age-old word takes us back to days when the written word was rare, and signatures and documents of little value; when what mattered in the conduct of human relationships was the oath, and the character of him who swore it. The covenant between men of honour, sanctified by religious language, solemn oath, and holy sacrifice, bound men in mutual loyalty for weal or woe. So Moses set forth the bond between Israel and her covenant-keeping God. "Which my covenant they brake," says Jeremiah; "but I will make a new covenant with the house of Israel, putting a new spirit within them, forgiving their iniquities, and writing my laws upon their hearts." "This cup," says Jesus, "is the cup of the New Covenant", established by the *oath* of Him who because He could swear by no greater, sware by Himself; established by the *character* of Him in whom is no variableness, nor shadow cast by changing phases; established yet again by the *precious blood* of Christ, as of a sacrifice without spot and without blemish. Every time we find the Table spread, and take into our unworthy hands the sacred cup, God is saying to us once more: "My covenant standeth sure, I am the Lord, I change not; I will never leave thee nor forsake thee. My covenant abides — does yours?"

The companionship of friends, the constancy of the cross, the covenant of grace — such are ways in which the Lord's Supper fortifies the soul. But one remains, the soul's secret contact with the risen, triumphant Lord. For everyone who truly worships at the Supper of our Lord, the Table becomes the extension through time of our own Damascus Road. We feel again His touch, His call, His amazing choice of us, and are constrained to answer, "Lord, what wilt thou have me to do?" This memorial service becomes another Upper Room where we may place our fingers in the print of the nails and know He is our Lord, and God. Every breaking of bread is another walk to Emmaus with a Lord triumphant, understanding, kind, and still commanding. Here lies the Lord's supreme intention: that we keep tryst with Him. He Himself invites us. Here He has made appointment to meet with us, and promised He shall be known of us in the breaking of bread. In this revitalising contact with a living Lord lies our deep sure comfort: "This do," He said, in remembrance of *me*."

29   The Signpost of the Soul

"Set thee up waymarks."
"Ye do show the Lord's death till he come."

Jeremiah 31:21, I Corinthians 11:26

How WELL the Master understood us! He knew the Christian way is long, and sometimes steep, and the spiritual weather changes. He understood the pressure of the world, and the soul's changing moods: how strait the gate and narrow the path, how easy for erring feet to go astray. As the prophet had suggested, people without waymarks are certain to get lost. And so the Lord ordained that at intervals along the Christian Way there should be set the signpost of the cross, marking the stages of our pilgrimage, making unmistakable our path. Time and again the invitation to His Table brings us back to stand beneath that cross and think afresh upon our spiritual journey.

Herein lies for most of us the great importance of regularly attending His Supper. To keep tryst with Jesus at His Table, not simply when we happen to feel inclined but at the stated intervals we have promised to observe, means that from time to time the cross will stand before us, a waymark on whatever road we may be travelling, to give us pause. G. K. Chesterton remarked that "the man who makes a vow makes an appointment with himself at some distant time or place". Our promise to commune is an appointment with our Lord beneath the cross, and keeping that appointment can mean all the difference between faithfulness and failure.

As the four limbs of the cross point up and down, to left and right, so the deep meanings of the Lord's Supper direct the soul's gaze, now one way, now another, in correction of our moods and enlargement of our view.

Sometimes the call to meet with the Lord at His Table finds us walking in shadows, uncertain of God, beset by doubts and faithless fears. Then *the signpost points us backwards,* down the long centuries to that Upper Room where Jesus Himself ordained this

139

impressive memorial of His passion. Our faith is rooted, this service seems to say, not in ourselves, our feelings, resolutions, or experiences; not in the eloquence of preachers or the persuasiveness of earnest evangelists, but in something God did, long ago, at Bethlehem, in Galilee, Judea, at Calvary.

Christianity is rooted, that is to say, in history. Without that history behind us, we who believe would be little more than sentimentalists blissfully wandering in a fog of make-believe. Instead, our feet are firmly planted on a superb story which no novel philosophy can deny, no science explain away, no changing mood of ours can alter or erase. We have a solid guarantee that God does love, given to us at Bethlehem; we possess a clear pattern for daily emulation, lived out for us in Galilee. We have received an unshakeable assurance of divine forgiveness, offered us at Calvary; we share an abiding conviction of immortality, implanted at the empty tomb. Here faith rests, on things God *did*; on things to which we can attach a date and place, events that are part of the history of the race.

There are periods of history, as there are moods of the soul, when that backward look may be all-important. In an age of change, of shaking of established things, some are continually afraid that new ideas, fresh discoveries, subtler arguments, may at any time blow Christian faith to the four winds! But the gospel is not mere philosophy, a cobweb system of human thought depending on the very slender threads of human wisdom: it is *news*, an account of historic happenings. Our faith is the interpretation, verified in experience, of something that did take place: "Christ Jesus came into the world to save sinners". That is written indelibly into the story of our world, and there are moments when our doubting hearts need nothing more urgently than to be pointed backwards to it.

> Lest I forget Gethsemane,
> Lest I forget Thine agony
> Lest I forget Thy love to me
> Lead me to Calvary.

Sometimes, however, the immediate need of Christian hearts is rather to take hope again, amid the gathered shadows of some personal disappointment, or because of the undermining sadness of some intimate bereavement, or possibly because the soul despairs of ever seeing Jesus crowned with glory and honour in a faithless world. Many are the causes of despondency that the heart discovers, or invents for itself; and it does appear with us as with Elijah, that the more jealous we have been for the cause of God the more likely we are at some time to sit in gloom and dark foreboding beneath our juniper.

If the invitation to the Lord's Supper find us there, *the signpost of the soul will point us forward* to the kingdom and the Coming. The triumphant expectation of a final act of God lies at the heart of the Supper. We celebrate the passion only "till he come"; we drink the wine that He is pledged to drink with us "in the Father's kingdom". As clearly as the Supper speaks of Him who was the Alpha, the Beginning, in whom the New Age came to be, just as clearly does it speak of Him who is Omega, the End of all things, in whom this age will find its consummation. And each returning memorial bids us look up, for our redemption draweth nigh.

The foundation of the Christian hope lies ultimately in the sovereignty of God and in the faithfulness of Christ: but its expression in the Lord's Supper lends a triple strength to our expectancy. First, because the hope of kingdom and advent is set against the darkness of rejection and defeat: to hope then, is to be able to hope at any time. Second, because the hope is set amid the weakness and failure of the twelve: not even their unpreparedness — or ours — can finally defeat God's sovereign will. And thirdly, because the hope is made to rest on something *God* will do, not something we are challenged to achieve. Challenge, and toil, and conflict certainly await us before the work is done: but the end is sure, and to that end, with all its glorious promise, the Lord's Table steadily directs our gaze.

Occasionally, the invitation to His Table finds us walking moodily alone, at odds with all our brethren, unhappy, and of little use to others, obsessed with our own affairs, turned inwards on ourselves. It may be we have much to cause anxiety; it may be there are things we cannot, or we dare not, share; it may be other folk have been unkind, or life itself has been unfair. There may be a dozen excuses we could frame to justify our self-concern. But then the returning days direct our steps to the Lord's Table, and we feel ashamed of our self-centredness.

For *the signpost points us outwards* from ourselves to the fellowship in which the Lord has set us, and beyond it to the world's pressing need. The Lord's Supper is essentially a shared experience, a covenant-meal, in which we break "one bread" and drink one cup. The Master's injunction rings in our ears, "Drink *ye all* of it" — and it cannot be obeyed in isolation. We cannot communicate alone. Inevitably the service links our little lives and their so limited concerns with the Church of Christ of all the past and all the world.

But even beyond the Church the signpost points: "Ye do show the Lord's death" is a significant phrase, for it means that each Supper service "proclaims, declares as does a herald" to a watching world the essence of the faith. As baptism is the public declaration of the great truth of regeneration, so the Lord's Supper is a public witness to the great truth of atonement. Though I come with lonely, self-attentive heart, I cannot stay that way: Communing with my Lord and His children sets me firmly in the wider fellowship of a living, onward-moving, witnessing community, to which I *do* belong.

And yet, at other times, *the signpost points us inwards.* It is possible, and perhaps for modern Christians it is usual, to become absorbed with outward things: many tasks demand attention, many issues claim our thought; we see the Christian life in terms of service, and are anxious to be busy for our Lord. It often happens that the inner life becomes neglected, and even in our busyness for Christ we lose the deep peace of His presence, the inspiration of His joy. Nor is it always zealous work and practical affairs that divert our thoughts from deeper things: for the world pulls and disobedience clouds the vision. Then too the Lord's Table bids us "judge ourselves" and challenges our "worthiness" to eat that bread and drink that cup. Whether we will or no, we are compelled to measure our spiritual progress and assess our loyalty, and having looked long within to look up again in penitence and prayer. Perhaps with most of us this is the direction oftenest needed and hardest to obey.

Backward, forward, outward and within: the Lord's Supper measures for us all the length and breadth, the height and depth of Christian life — and of the love of Christ.

30 The Focus of Remembrance

"This do for a remembrance."

I Corinthians 11:24

THE DESIRE to be remembered has been the mark of all great souls in every generation. It has shaped the art, the architecture, and the customs of every significant age. Prompted by it, men built the Pyramids to perpetuate the glories of their kings, set up stone pillars bearing famous names, erected piles of stones beside the roads, inscribed the rocks, carved lovely statues, guarded graves and designed elaborate and costly tombs.

Solemn festivals preserved the tribal memories; tellers of tales were honoured for their stories of the past; poets sang of the exploits of old time, and long and laborious books were written to keep remembered things alive. Great indeed is the effort, and skill and fervour that have gone to rob the past of its oblivion and prolong — if only in thought — the life of men.

Behind the desire there lies a valid insight. Without memory, life is dull, and foolish, and very superficial; without memory there can be no wisdom, no profit from experience, no education and no progress. Age without memories is very lonely; sorrow without memories must be very bitter; adversity without memories of God's faithfulness in the past, is bereft of courage and of hope. To be forgotten is a form of humiliation among the hardest for the heart to bear, and the warning that the memory of the wicked will be cut off grows more solemn as you think of it.

Forgetfulness is not just a humorous failing, it is folly, and sometimes worse. For short memories make for shallow souls, and empty minds; mistakes are repeated from generation to generation, and with the Hebrew Preacher men come to feel that "all is vanity . . . there is no remembrance of the former things". In John Buchan's haunting phrase, "Memory holds the door" — to many things essential to a truly human life: thankfulness, insight, friendship, strength of purpose, understanding, appreciation, and character.

Especially character. For only those who keep in mind the

143

prayers that have been answered, the battles won, the sins forgiven, reveal the precious trinity of qualities that endear great
souls — humility, gratitude and courage. Only those who remember learn the secret of turning the past to good account, making
each failure the spur to greater effort, each success the impulse
to new zeal, each personal sorrow the spring of readier sympathy,
each sin the challenge to watch and pray.

Doubtless it is true that those souls grow who reach continually
forwards to what is so far unattained. But equally is it true that
those whose memories reach far back to harvest all the lessons of
experience carry forward with them riches not to be discovered
otherwise.

It is this moral value of remembrance that lends importance to
the Bible's oft-repeated warning to "remember. . ." . How often
Israel is enjoined to keep in mind her days of servitude, to remember what God did to Pharaoh, to recall the way the Lord had
led her, to bear within her heart the day that she came out of
Egypt, the word that Moses spake, the mercies she had known,
and above all, her Creator. All the values of spiritual experience are
lost without remembrance, and God's might and mercy may as
well not have been if we forget. There lies the explanation of
many a stunted soul.

With these things in our mind, the human, the moral and the
spiritual significance of memory, we listen more carefully to the
words of Christ's command: "This do, for a remembrance". As
though He feared we might forget Him, Jesus provided against
the peril and impoverishment a lapse of memory would entail,
by ordaining a commemoration, with symbols of His body and
His blood, to keep remembrance green. And wonderfully does
His Supper serve that end.

Here, at the Table, and beneath the cross, we cannot but *remember our conversion*. Sometimes we are tempted to move
on, not in the sense of genuine spiritual progress, but as moving
away from that humbling memory of a day when sin-laden and
repentant we knelt before the cross for mercy. The New Testament will not let us leave that memory entirely behind. "Where-
fore remember . . . ye were without Christ . . . aliens . . . strang-
ers . . . without hope" is Paul's counsel; and again, listing the

144

sins of paganism, he adds, "Remember . . . such were some of you".

Peter explains the reason for this reminder of unhappier days. He that lacketh the marks of spiritual progress "is blind, and cannot see afar off, and hath forgotten that he was purged from his old sins". Lack of progress, lack of foresight, of watchfulness, arise — the apostle who denied his Lord contends — from sheer forgetfulness. So the letter to the Hebrews, too, desires the readers to "call to mind the former days when they were enlightened, and received the heavenly gift" that they might find the courage to endure. The evergreen memory of God's amazing mercy to ourselves, repeatedly renewed at each Lord's Supper, is a constant source of wonder, zeal, and love.

Here at the Table, too, we cannot but *remember the cost* of our salvation. The broken bread brings vividly before us the agony He endured; the poured red wine speaks eloquently of life surrendered to make atonement for our sin. Emphatically, we are not our own. Equally emphatically, we did not save ourselves. Strange though it may seem, we tend to overlook both things as the years slip by; use, familiarity, carelessness quickly dull the memory.

Looking backwards through the years that we have followed Christ, we find it easy to suppose that by our idealism and faith, our strenuous conflict and our service, we built up our own experience, and fashioned our own Christian character. The literal truth about us all is that but for His prevenient mercy, we could have accomplished nothing: ideals, faith, conflict, service — all were out of reach until He lifted us, mere words until He gave us life.

> *And every virtue we possess*
> *And every conflict won*
> *And every thought of holiness*
> *Are His alone.*

Because we forget this, we tend to take our life again into our own hands, though once in eager faith and consecration we surrendered it to Christ. Here at His Table we remember we are the Lord's. His body was broken, His brow was torn, His lips were parched, His hands and feet were pierced, His heart was broken that *my* body might become His temple, my mind His

145

instrument, my lips His mouthpiece, my hands and feet His tools, my heart His throne. Body for body He has purchased mine that I should yield my members as instruments of righteousness to Him.

This the broken bread still says to us, in words of the apostle: "I beseech you therefore brethren, by the mercies of God, that ye present your bodies, a *living* sacrifice, holy, acceptable unto God; which is your reasonable service". So too the cup: life for life He purchased mine, my days and months and years, my strength and gifts and loyalty; *consider* the words —

> *Were the whole realm of nature mine,*
> *That were a present far too small:*
> *Love so amazing, so divine,*
> *Demands my soul, my life, my all.*

Remembering what my salvation cost my Lord, like David I dare not offer unto the Lord of that which cost me nothing.

And here at the Table, obviously, we cannot but *remember* Christ. "This do," He said, "in remembrance of me." To the two disciples at Emmaus, He was known in the breaking of bread: so is He still. Again and again He will reveal Himself to us, as with reverent faith and quickened memory we fulfil His word, and seek Him in the bread and wine. We shall see Him as the *covenanting Christ*, pledging Himself to see us through all coming days, and not to fail. We shall see Him as the *commanding Christ*, laying upon us all His will — to love one another, bear more fruit, abide in Him, and let His words abide in us, to love Him and treasure His commandments.

We shall see Him as the *coming Christ*, assuring us of the fulfilment of His work in the kingdom of His Father. And we shall see Him, here at the Table, as the *continuing Christ* — for this is why we *must* remember Him. He walks beside us, and our eyes must not be holden. He stands behind us, and we must not mistake Him for another. He waits upon our shore, and we may miss Him if we dare forget His face. He sits beside us at the Table waiting to show again His hands and side. At each memorial celebration we must welcome Him afresh, take Him anew as Saviour, Friend, Redeemer, Lord, lest even in the symbols of the service we forget the Lord.

According to Thy gracious word,
In meek humility,
This will I do, my dying Lord,
I will remember Thee.

And when these failing lips grow dumb
And mind and memory flee,
When Thou shalt in Thy kingdom come,
Jesus, remember me.

31 The Bread of Life

"I am the bread of life: he that cometh to me shall never hunger."
"Take, eat; this is my body."

John 6:35, Matthew 26:26

IT IS PERHAPS too much to ask that the essential things of life should also be romantic. Necessities are rarely exciting until they are scarce: then the dullest everyday requirement can focus our entire attention. Bread, for example, may be the veriest symbol of drabness; in times of famine it becomes the foremost, universal, unparalleled goal of millions.

In both respects, as that which is ordinary and necessary, and as that which may become priceless, bread is the natural symbol of a hunger deeper than that for food. In famous words of Studdert Kennedy:

> *The hunger in man's heart is infinite*
> *And craves infinity for food.*
> *I dare not give him bread unless I give him more:*
> *He must have God.*

For man, assuredly, shall not live by bread alone. Deep within the human spirit lie instinctive appetites which material welfare cannot satisfy. Man hungers to be good in spite of evil propensities; to understand the meaning of things in face of life's perplexities; to be comforted amid his manifold adversities. He longs for peace, for righteousness, for inspiration, for truth, for hope. He wishes desperately to be sure that the universe is friendly. He hungers for God.

All of which reveals a nature too complex to be sustained merely as the beasts around him: to deny that hunger is to dehumanise the race. Man is something more than a cupful of chemicals in marvellous combination; life is more than a laboratory experiment: and for lack of the infinite, intangible, sustenance of the spirit, many a modern soul is starved.

When that happens, in any generation, or phase of society, all lovelier things weaken and die, and individuals become aware, though vaguely, of intense dissatisfaction at levels they but dimly understand, and cannot explain. An ancient prophet described a familiar modern experience in a phrase that sets the teeth on edge: "He feedeth on ashes".

Spiritual hunger certainly exists, but it need never go unsatisfied. "Blessed are they that hunger and thirst after righteousness, for *they shall be filled.*" Christ offers Himself to men under many metaphors, but that of Bread of Life is at once one of the simplest and most meaningful, and one of the richest and most apt.

Behind the claim, a threefold level of meaning may be discerned. Jesus had taught and travelled a long day in Galilee, and the crowd had stayed far into the evening. There at a picnic-meal on the hillside high above the lake, a vast multitude had been fed with five loaves and a pair of fish. Every miracle, in John's eyes, is also a "sign": Jesus had come to a spiritually hungry, heart-starved world as the "Bread of God" who nourishes and satisfies. He who is the Water for man's thirst, the Light for man's darkness, the Good Shepherd for man's wandering, is also Bread for man's hunger, in whom is life, and the means of sustaining it. A weary, footsore world, far from home and nourishment, may turn in its emergency to feed its starving soul upon the Christ of God and find *life.*

The next day, in the synagogue at Capernaum across the lake, the preacher is Christ: the text, the miracle of the night before: the point under discussion, the difference between the meat that perisheth and that which endures unto life eternal. But an argument develops. Hecklers demand to know if Christ compares Himself with the great Moses who likewise fed the people in the wilderness, providing manna not on one summer evening only, but throughout the long, hot, torturing march from Egypt to Canaan.

Our Lord accepts the significant comparison. But He claims superiority: first, because He Himself like the manna (but unlike Moses) "came down from heaven"; secondly, because those who ate of Moses' manna are long since dead, but those who feed on Christ shall live for ever. Here, a wholly new turn is given to the conception. The manna was daily food for a daily journey, and Jesus claims likewise to be the continuing sustenance of those who follow Him. But whereas manna, and bread, nourishes the life already possessed. Christ the living Bread *confers* life on those who take of Him, imparting life eternal. "If any man eat of this bread he shall live forever." He is our manna for the desert journey, and our "new corn" in the heavenly Canaan.

But John wrote neither on the hillside nor in the synagogue, but long afterwards, and a third level of meaning emerges in his reflection, through the Galilean story, of half a century of Christian experience. No one can doubt that John's later knowledge of the Christian Supper has influenced his telling of the story. Into the argument about the picnic-meal, there creeps an emphasis upon "the bread which is my flesh, which I will give for the life of the world" and a reference to drinking Christ's blood. "Except ye eat the flesh of the Son of man and drink his blood ye have no life in you. Whoso eateth my flesh and drinketh my blood hath eternal life. . . . For my flesh is meat indeed, and my blood is drink indeed."

John has seen a deeper, prophetic meaning in the Capernaum sermon. To him, the evening miracle on the hillside seems a kind of rehearsal for a darker drama in the Upper Room, where Jesus again took bread, gave thanks, and gave to His disciples, saying, "Take, eat, this is my body, broken for you".

To take the glowing words in some materialist, literalist way, is to misconstrue them utterly, and to lose their depth of meaning. In Capernaum, as He spoke, and again in the Upper Room beside the Table, He stood there, amongst them, the living Jesus. "I am the living bread," He said, and added a warning against superstitious or materialist misunderstanding. "It is the spirit that quickeneth; the flesh profiteth nothing: the words that I speak unto you they are spirit, and they are life." The spirit and the words impart the life.

Christ is *Bread*, as He is Water or Vine, or Door, or Shepherd — figuratively. Jesus is talking in symbols, but He is talking serious, important, vital truth without which the Lord's Supper and our Christian life is impoverished and starved. Christ Himself, the living Christ, is the Nourisher of life, the Sustainer of the spirit, the Vine from which we draw the soul's replenishment, the Manna upon which we live, the Bread of life, given, broken, shared, on whom we feed.

Given: "For the bread of God is he which cometh down from

heaven, and giveth life unto the world." The life of man is never self-sustaining, it is nourished at its source. Even our devotions — Bible-reading, worship, work, seasons of prayer, the Lord's Supper — will fail us unless they are more than our "spiritual exercises", and involve a real and personal laying hold of the divine provision for our need, feeding, day by day, upon the Lord Himself, living, dead and risen.

Broken: "The bread that I will give is my flesh, which I will give for the life of the world. . . . Take, eat; this is my body, broken for you." For as the loaf cannot satisfy or nourish while it remains whole upon the table, so Christ the Bread of life had first to be taken, in wicked hands, and broken by sinful men — that He might impart to all the life that was in Him for men.

Shared: The Bread, says Jesus repeatedly, must be "eaten". It is necessary that by some means the soul appropriates the Christ: and the means are not left undefined. According to John's record Jesus speaks in this connection of "seeing the Son", of "coming to me", of "believing on me" as well as of "eating my flesh".

These are the several stages of spiritual appropriation: to recognise who Christ is and what He does; to approach in longing and in penitence the Christ we recognise; then to rest the soul in confidence and trust upon Christ; and thereafter to lay hold of Him by every energy of faith and prayer, of love and loyalty, to the end.

> *Bread of heaven! on Thee I feed,*
> *For Thy flesh is meat indeed;*
> *Ever may my soul be fed*
> *With this true and living Bread;*
> *Day by day with strength supplied,*
> *Through the life of Him who died.*

How oft we come, soul hungry, to the Lord's Table: longing for strength, eager for refreshment, hungering for righteousness and joy and hope. Jesus said, "He that eateth me, shall live by me. . . . Take, eat: this is my body".

"The Body of our Lord, Jesus Christ, which was given for thee, preserve thy body and soul unto everlasting life. Take and eat this in remembrance that Christ died for thee, and feed on him in thy heart by faith with thanksgiving."

32 The Cup of the Covenant

"I appoint unto you . . . that ye may eat and drink at my table in my kingdom."
"This is my blood of the new covenant."

Luke 22:29-30, Matthew 26:28

It is usual nowadays to smile indulgently at medieval stories of knights sworn to noble deeds and damsels forever needing rescue from distress. A great deal of water has drained from the moats of ancient castles since that age of chivalry, and we are proud of our progress from feudalism to the factory. Yet for whole generations, those knightly tales enshrined the loftiest ideals of Christian faith, and chief among them the undying search for the sacred chalice of the Last Supper — the "quest of the Holy Grail".

The original cup was brought to Britain, so the legend ran, by Joseph of Arimathea, and thence taken to heaven. To be allowed sight of it was the highest goal of Christian manhood, the badge of honour and the crown of valour. The vision of the Holy Grail was heaven's own seal upon courage, purity of heart, and saintliness.

> *Ah blessed vision! blood of God!*
> *My spirit beats her mortal bars,*
> *As down dark tides the glory slides*
> *And star-like mingles with the stars.*
>
> *Then move the trees, the copses nod,*
> *Wings flutter, voices hover clear:*
> *O just and faithful knight of God*
> *Ride on! the prize is near.*
>
> *So pass I hostel, hall, and grange;*
> *By bridge and ford, by park and pale*
> *All-armed I ride, whate'er betide*
> *Until I find the Holy Grail.*

It is all very old-world and heart-stirring: but what matters to us is, that beneath this mingling of history and fairy-tale lie accurate and moving insights into the deepest meanings of that cup of sacred memory.

For three things mark the knight of the Holy Grail in medieval romance. He is dedicated to "break the heathen and uphold the Christ", and the sacred chalice is symbol of that Christian salvation he would establish everywhere. He must "ride abroad redressing human wrongs", winning the wayward by deeds of mercy and delivering the oppressed — the chalice symbolising suffering with and for others. And he is essentially a man under oath to his king, scorning to break faith or fail his pledged word, because the chalice symbolises covenanted honour and fidelity. And in these three things the meaning of the cup is faithfully expressed.

"What shall I render unto the Lord for all his benefits toward me? I will take the *cup of salvation. . . .*" The cup of His Table is certainly that; a cup of salvation.

The ancient ritual of sacrifice frequently included a sacred meal, with solemn pouring out of wine as offering to God, and drinking together in honour of the festival. David speaks of the Lord, "spreading a table before me . . . my cup running over". The idea passed into Messianic prophecy as the Messianic banquet, when men shall come from all quarters to sit with Abraham, Isaac and Jacob at God's table. Someone said to Jesus, Blessed is he that shall eat bread in the kingdom of God; and Jesus replied with the story of the Great Supper, the feast of the kingdom.

For life under God's rule is a banquet. It is a wedding feast to which God in mercy invites us: the water of life is changed to wine, the "new wine" of the kingdom. "Ye shall eat and drink at my table in my kingdom"; ye "shall hunger no more, neither thirst any more"; indeed men shall consider you intoxicated — as at Pentecost — for the fullness of joy that is yours. For the cup of His Table is a cup of full salvation, rich, royal and satisfying: a festal cup of joy and deep fulfilment.

This is Christ's meaning when He promises to drink it new, with us, in His Father's kingdom. The note of gladness and of thankfulness must not be omitted from the solemn service of remembrance. It is a "cup of blessing" we bless; it is with thanksgiving that we celebrate; this is wine that maketh glad the hearts of all men who believe. "Christ our Passover is sacrificed for us: let us keep festival."

But the cup of His passion is nevertheless a *cup of suffering,* which they who first drank of it, and we who follow, are called to share with Christ. "Ye shall indeed drink of the cup that I drink of", the cup, as so often in the Old Testament, of affliction, tears and agony. The waters of a full cup were wrung out to Him, mingled with gall and bitterness.

"O my Father, if it be possible, let this cup pass from me," the discipless heard Him pray, not long after He had said to them, "Drink ye all, of it". For the cup of His Table symbolised, beneath the joy of assured salvation, the call to share His burden with Him, and bear His cross. We too are Christian knights, challenged to dare, do battle, and suffer for our Lord, till the task is done, the enemy defeated, and the price is paid that sets men free.

For modern Christians this implication of discipleship is made unforgettable by one name — Albert Schweitzer. Among the motives, gratitude, compassion, atonement, that underlie his renunciation of academic fame and sent him to the labour and sacrifice of Lambaréné, prominent is the impulse to take seriously the command of Jesus: "Out of the depths of my feeling of happiness there grew up gradually within me an understanding of the saying of Jesus that we must not treat our lives as being for ourselves alone. Whoever is spared personal pain must feel himself called to help diminish the pain of others. We must all carry our share of the misery which lies upon the world. . . . To those who obey Him . . . He will reveal Himself, in the toils, the conflicts, the sufferings which they shall pass through in His fellowship."

That surely is the challenge, and the promise, renewed each time we take the cup of His passion into our hands.

Once more, the cup of the Lord's Supper is nonetheless the *cup of the new covenant.* By ancient custom, drinking together, or to each other's "health", constitutes a pledge of friendship, an expression of goodwill. Probably the exchange of food, the drinking of offered wine, originally expressed trust in the one who offered it — that the good things were not poisoned! Possibly too ideas of eating and drinking a curse upon broken faith lie behind the covenant-cup. However that be, at some time in Jewish history covenant-wine had been added to the lamb and bitter herbs of Passover ritual, strengthening its memories of the covenant-sacrifice, and covenant-meal, when Moses read the law in the hearing of the people, and on their pledge of obedience sealed with sprinkled blood the covenant with God.

Yet Israel failed to keep her word. Jeremiah promised a renewal of the covenant, when God would freely forgive the broken oath, place His law within their hearts, and be known of all, from least to greatest. This is the covenant inaugurated in the Upper Room in "the cup of a new covenant in [Christ's] blood".

The *basis* of that covenant is God's redeeming act in Christ. Its *terms* are man's obedience and faith, God's promise of forgiveness, blessing, and eternal life. Its *guarantee* is the blood of Jesus and the pledged word of God that nothing shall separate us from His love. Its *strength* lies in the steadfast, timeless unchangeableness of God, who in Moses made covenant with His people and was disappointed, in Jeremiah offered again and found no response, and in Jesus seeks yet once more to bind us to Himself as He bound Himself to us at Calvary.

Thus we too are men under solemn oath, pledged to our Lord the King as with invisible bonds that every Lord's Supper strengthens, in a covenant of blood more enduring than steel. Weak, wayward, vacillating, wistful, we in ourselves are as unreliable and unready as that little band who first passed the cup from hand to hand: but we rely not on our strength of purpose, or our oft-broken promise, but on His might and mercy. And here, at the Table, once again, knowing all there is to know about our failures and our faults, He still renews His pledge to see us through. "This is my blood of the new covenant: drink — *all of you* — of it."

33 The Promise of the End

"Until that day. . . ."
. . . "Till he come."

Matthew 26:29, I Corinthians 11:26

G. F. WATT's familiar painting, entitled "Hope", was severely criticised on its first appearance, as more fitted to express despair than hopefulness; and the painter was rebuked for altogether too gloomy a view of life and of the world.

This was because his painting shows a lonely, sad, and wistful figure, seated drooping and downcast above the globe of the world, against a dark, forbidding sky, but one star faintly visible. The figure's eyes are bandaged, and she caresses with melancholy fingers a broken lute, on which one solitary string remains.

This said the critics is not Hope: this is pessimism, and blindness, and despair. Hope should stride the dawn with trumpets blowing and birdsong, and opening buds, for Hope is youthful, gay and confident!

But people thought again, and, as often happens, saw that the artist had thought too. For the moments when hope matters, when our hearts and hands reach out for something to cling to, to wait for, to live towards, are just the moments when things have gone wrong; when the sky is dark, the stars are going out, the strings are breaking; when the light and the music die away, and sight itself is denied and we sit in gathering darkness.

Then all our hope gathers in any one star that still gleams, any one string that still murmurs promises. We never know the value, or the necessity, or the moral meaning, of hope in God, until the darkness falls, and we feel alone and cannot see our way.

Then, as Paul says truly, again linking the virtue with its appropriate situation, we are *saved* by hope. So too Jesus calls for the heroism of hopefulness when the days are darkening and the storm sets in: "There shall be signs in the sun, and in the moon, . . . and upon the earth distress of nations, with perplexity: the sea and the waves roaring; men's hearts failing them for fear, and for looking after those things which are coming on the earth . . . and when these things come to pass, then look up, and lift up your heads; for your redemption draweth nigh".

Obviously there is more here, in the association of Christian hope with danger, and darkness and dread, than just a dramatic effect, a mere contrast of light and shade. It *is* in such times, in personal experience of sorrow or fear or great anxiety, and in times of wider distress, and peril and foreboding, that Hope comes into her own — and so often saves the soul. Hope, after all, is part of the armour of the Christian: equipment for conflict.

Surely, that is why nothing in the whole circle of Christian worship, not the *Sursum Corda* of the ancient liturgy, nor the recurring season of Advent — nothing so stirs the Christian's hope as the service of the Lord's Supper. Because here, against the background of gloom and fear, of division and unpreparedness, of sorrow and betrayal and the threat of death, and the Lord's solemn warning of peril and temptation — against all this Jesus speaks so calmly of the future.

With the bread broken in His hands to prefigure the breaking of His body and wine poured to show the shedding of His blood, He still looks forward confidently: "Until that day . . . . with you . . . . My Father's kingdom . . . . the Father's house". Right through the memorial feast there throbs the expectation of good things still to come.

It has been suggested that under foreign oppression, since the Exile, the Jews had found new meanings in the ancient Passover, and celebrated the deliverance from Egypt with one eye, so to speak, on the future, when God should effect another deliverance from Roman rule, and a greater than Moses would appear to lead Israel into freedom. Certainly, at Passovertide, the breath of freedom was in the air, and the Romans were more than ever watchful, and nervous.

Jesus seems to hint at something of promise in the festival: for He says He had desired to eat the Passover with the disciples before He suffered; and He would not eat of it again *until it be fulfilled* in the Kingdom of God. That is one note of hope at the heart of the Lord's Supper: the promise of a new redemption, a yet more glorious Passover deliverance.

A second is the note of resurrection, of life, and renewed fellowship. "I will drink *with you*" is His promise at the Table. According to John, He added, "A little while, and ye shall not see me: and again, a little while, and ye shall see me. . . " . And on the way to Olivet immediately afterwards He says, "After I am risen, I will go before you into Galilee".

Thus at the crisis of peril He could speak, not of death only, and His body and His blood: but of *life*, assured, unbroken, and unending. "I go. . . . I will come again . . . . and abide with you."

The third note of hope is that of triumph. Before the battle was joined, before the foe was met, Jesus talked calmly of victory. "This, *thy* day," He said to Jerusalem; "this is your hour" He was to say to the Temple guards. But here at the Table He looks beyond the immediate day and hour — to *"that* day". And "that day" was the day when "the kingdom shall come", the day of the Father's rule — not Caiaphas' or Caesar's or Satan's, but "my Father's".

Certainly there was little sign of triumph as the plots thickened about Him and the hour of His agony approached. But His heart did not doubt the issue: the Father would reign, and the will of God be done. So could they hope on in the darkness, and take heart. For the Messianic banquet would be spread; their cup would run over; there would be welcome and rejoicing in the great supper of the King, in "that day". And He *would* drink with them, in the Father's kingdom.

The fourth note of hope sounded at the Table is the prevision of glory. "I go unto my Father. . . . Let not your heart be troubled . . . in my Father's house are many mansions. . . . I go to prepare a place for you . . .that where I am ye may be also." The very name Father implies a final gathering home. Here, too, the reference to the covenant is important: for the covenant long promised is an *everlasting* covenant; it holds for life eternal. Our Hope is "entered into that which is within the veil": the "Forerunner" to prepare ahead for us. Thus every recurring Lord's Supper speaks to us again, in the shadow of the cross, of the crown of glory laid up for all those that love His appearing.

And that appearing is the fifth note of hope in the Christian Supper: "I will come again"; it is only "till he come". John, you will remember, gathers up in one glorious picture all the majesty and pathos of this theme, as he sees in heaven the throne of God, and in the hand of God the sealed book of the future which no man in heaven or earth is worthy to take and open. Until the Lamb, a lamb as it had been slain, comes forward to take the book from the hand of God, and amid the adoration of all the hosts of heaven to break one by one the seals and unroll the coming years, till the kingdoms of this world become the kingdoms of our God and of His Christ, and He shall reign for ever and ever.

Let us not imagine it is harder for us to hold that steadying, courageous hope than it was for John. He faced Caesar, and death. Yet John knew that the Table calls us, again and yet again, to renew our confidence that Jesus shall come, shall reign. In the Upper Room the Master had not merely bade farewell and urged them to *remember*: He also bade them hope, and wait, and watch, for His appearing.

Thus the service of the Lord's Supper sounds out the fivefold chord of Christian hope — of deliverance, of risen life, of victory for the kingdom, of glory ahead, and of His coming.

> *Tarry no longer; toward thine heritage*
> *Haste on thy way, and be of right good cheer.*
> *Go each day onward on thy pilgrimage;*
> *And think how short a time thou shalt bide here.*

For here, we have no continuing city: we do not entirely "belong"; our hearts are in another homeland. Sailing as mariners towards another shore, we navigate, not only by the harbours and the landmarks left behind us, and the stars set overhead, but by the lights and landfall on a distant horizon. Each memorial service marks a stage of the journey home. The Master says to us again across the Table against the background of *all* fears, sorrows, toil and disappointment, "Look up, lift up your heads, for your redemption draweth nigh".

> *And thus that dark betrayal night*
> *With the last advent we unite,*
> *By one blest chain of loving rite*
> *Until He come.*

> *Oh blessed hope! with this elate,*
> *Let not our hearts be desolate,*
> *But strong in faith, in patience wait*
> *Until He come.*

159